WOMEN'S EMANCIPATION DURING THE PROPHET'S LIFETIME

MUSLIM WOMEN'S PARTICIPATION IN PROFESSIONAL, SOCIAL AND POLITICAL LIFE

Volume 3

Abd al-Halim Abu Shuqqah

Translated and Edited by
Adil Salahi

KUBE
PUBLISHING

Muslim Women's Participation in professional, Social and Political Life, volume 3

First published in England by
Kube Publishing Ltd
Markfield Conference Centre,
Ratby Lane, Markfield,
Leicestershire, LE67 9SY,
United Kingdom
Tel: +44 (0) 1530 249230
Fax: +44 (0) 1530 249656
Email: info@ kubepublishing.com
Website: www.kubepublishing.com

WOMEN'S EMANCIPATION DURING THE PROPHET'S LIFETIME

CIP data for this book is available from the British Library.

ISBN: 978-1-84774-169-1 *Paperback*
ISBN: 978-1-84774-170-7 *Ebook*

Translate and Edit by: Adil Salahi
Cover Design by: Nasir Cadir
Typeset by: nqaddoura@hotmail.com
Printed by: Elma Basim, Turkey

Contents

Transliteration Table

Consonants. Arabic

initial, unexpressed, medial and final: ء ʾ

ا	a	د	d	ض	ḍ	ك	k
ب	b	ذ	dh	ط	ṭ	ل	l
ت	t	ر	r	ظ	ẓ	م	m
ث	th	ز	z	ع	ʿ	ن	n
ج	j	س	s	غ	gh	هـ	h
ح	ḥ	ش	sh	ف	f	و	w
خ	kh	ص	ṣ	ق	q	ي	y

Vowels, diphthongs, etc.

short:	ـَ	a	ـِ	i	ـُ	u
long:	ـَا	ā	ـُو	ū	ـِي	ī
diphthongs:			ـَوْ	aw		
			ـَيْ	ay		

CHAPTER I

Women in Professional Work

Examples from the Prophet's Time

Muslim women prefer to conduct their lives enlightened by the guidance God revealed in His Book, the Qur'an, and illustrated by His Messenger. The practical examples we will provide occur in the Qur'an and the sunnah in reference to particular situations. If we were to list all the practical examples that took place during earlier prophets' lifetimes, as well as during Prophet Muhammad's lifetime, these will only give us some practical cases of the implementation of such guidance. There is, however, a much wider area for such implementation not only in our own generation but also for future generations. Indeed, there can be numerous situations, provided by different social set-ups, that adhere to divine guidance.

The reader will not fail to notice that we include in our discussions, cases where women worked as volunteers. We make no apologies for this. The fact is that God, the Law-Giver, has permitted mixing between men and women in such work. Whether the work gives financial remuneration or not is immaterial. Our study is concerned with proving that such mixing is permissible, according to need. Let us, then outline the areas of women's work during the Prophet's lifetime:

Breast-feeding Children

God says in the Qur'an: "Let them dwell wherever you dwell, according to your means, and do not harass them so as to make their lives a misery. If they are with child, maintain them until they have delivered their burden. If, after that, they suckle your infants, pay them for it. Take counsel with one another in a fair manner. If some of you make things difficult, let another woman suckle the child." (65: 6)

It should be noted that this verse relates to divorced women. If a woman is divorced during her pregnancy or after child birth and suckles her child, she is entitled to be paid by the child's father, i.e. her ex-husband, for so doing. The amount is agreed by mutual counsel and in a fair manner, as the verse states.

Anas ibn Mālik quotes the Prophet as saying: "'A child was born to me last night and I called him Ibrāhīm, after my first ancestor.' He then gave the child to Umm Sayf, the wife of a blacksmith called Abu Sayf, for breast-feeding..." Another version also narrated by Anas states: "I have never seen anyone who is more compassionate when dealing with young children than God's Messenger (peace be upon him). His son, Ibrāhīm, was given to a wet nurse in the high areas of Madinah for breast-feeding. The Prophet used to go there, and we would go with him. He used to go in, even though the house was full of smoke, take the child and kiss him before going back. The breast-feeding woman's husband was a blacksmith." (Related by Muslim)

A Shepherd

Saʿd ibn Muʿādh narrated that a slave girl belonging to Kaʿb ibn Mālik tended sheep by Mount Salʿ. One day a sheep was critically injured. The girl managed to get to it whilst it was still alive. She then slaughtered the sheep using a sharp stone. The Prophet was asked about this case and he said: 'You can eat it.' (Related by al-Bukhari)

Commenting on the hadith that mentions Maymūnah, the Prophet's wife, and her freeing a slave girl she had, Ibn Ḥajar says that the version related by al-Nasā'ī quotes the Prophet as saying to her: "Would it not have been better that you should have given her to free your niece from tending sheep?"[1]

In Agriculture

Jābir ibn 'Abdullāh reports: "My aunt was divorced. She wanted to go and gather her dates. A man reproached her for wanting to go out. She went to the Prophet and told him. He said to her: 'Yes, you can gather your fruit. It may be that you will give something as charity or do some other good work.'" [Related by Muslim]

Jābir reports that the Prophet visited Umm Mubashshir, a woman from the Anṣār, when she was on her date farm. He asked her: "Were these palm date trees planted by a Muslim person or by an unbeliever?" She said they were planted by a Muslim. He said: "If a Muslim plants a tree or some other plant and a human being or an animal or any creature eats of it, it will count for him as an act of charity." (Related by Muslim)

Handicraft

Zaynab, 'Abdullāh ibn Mas'ūd's wife, reports: "I was in the mosque when the Prophet said to women, 'Give generously to charity, even

---

1. In other versions of this hadith, the Prophet said to his wife that she could have earned greater reward by giving the slave girl to her maternal uncles. This version explains the reason. Her uncles were poor and their own daughter had to tend the sheep. Had his wife, Maymūnah, given the slave to them, she would have been attending their sheep instead of their own daughter.

if some of your jewellery.'" Zaynab used to support 'Abdullāh and some orphan children under her care. She said to her husband: "Ask God's Messenger whether my support of you and those orphans can be offset against my zakat dues." (Related by al-Bukhari and Muslim) Another version related by Ibn Mājah mentions that 'she was a craftswoman'. A third version given in Ibn Sa'd's *al-Ṭabaqāt al-Kubrā* states: "'Abdullāh ibn Mas'ūd's wife who was the mother of his children was a craftswoman. She said to the Prophet: 'Messenger of God, I have a skill and I sell what I make. My husband, my children and myself have nothing else. How about my support of them?' The Prophet said to her: 'You will earn a reward for whatever you spend in supporting them.'"

Management

Jābir ibn 'Abdullāh reports that an Anṣārī woman said to the Prophet: "... I have a slave who is a carpenter..." Another version adds: "She instructed her slave and he cut wood from certain trees and made a pulpit..." (Related by al-Bukhari)

In this context we may remind the reader that Umm Sharīk, a Companion of the Prophet, opened her home for guests, and she often received guests from among the early migrants, i.e. the *Muhājirīn*, from Makkah. This was akin to making her home a guest house, but in a voluntary way.

Nursing

'Ā'ishah reports: "Sa'd ibn Mu'ādh was injured during the siege of Madinah when a man from the Quraysh called Ḥabbān ibn al-'Arafah, hit him with an arrow cutting a vein in his arm.[2] The Prophet ordered that a tent should be erected in the mosque so that he could visit him... There was also a tent used by the Ghifārī people in the

2. This vein was called *al-akḥal*, a main artery, and when it was cut, bleeding could not be stopped.

mosque. They were suddenly alarmed when they saw blood seeping through to their tent. They asked: 'You, people in the tent! What is this seeping through from your side?' It was Sa'd as his wound had reopened and he was bleeding heavily. He died because of this injury. May God be pleased with him." (Related by al-Bukhari)

Explaining the point of the tent belonging to the Ghifār tribe, Ibn Ḥajar says: "We quoted earlier Ibn Isḥāq saying that the tent belonged to Rufaydah who belonged to the tribe of Aslam. It may be that her husband was from Ghifār... The Prophet gave instructions to nurse Sa'd in Rufaydah's tent at his mosque. She used to nurse the wounded. The Prophet said: 'Put him in her tent so that I can easily visit him.'"

Ibn Ḥajar also explains the hadith reported by Umm 'Aṭiyyah: "We used to attend the sick and nurse the wounded." He says: "This hadith tells us that it is permissible for a woman to nurse men who are not her relatives, bringing them medication and looking after them, without touching them except when needed and in safe situations."

Anas ibn Mālik reports that the Prophet allowed an Anṣārī family to be treated of a scorpion's bite and ear ache by saying certain prayers." (Related by al-Bukhari and Muslim) The reference in the hadith is to the women in this Anṣārī family.

The following hadith is included in al-Albānī's *Silsilat al-Aḥādīth al-Ṣaḥīḥah*, [i.e. Anthology of Authentic Hadiths]: "A man from the Anṣār was suffering from an illness that caused skin cuts to appear on the sides of his body. People told him that al-Shifā' bint 'Abdullāh was known to heal this illness through supplication to God. He went to her and requested her help. She said: 'By God, I have not used such supplication to heal anyone since I became a Muslim.' The Anṣārī man went to the Prophet and reported to him what happened. The

Prophet sent for her. When she came, he asked her to tell him the full wording of the supplication she used. She did so. He then said to her: 'Use this supplication and teach it to Ḥafṣah [his wife] just as you taught her how to write.'"[3] (Related by al-Hakim)

Serving the Army

Al-Rubayyiʿ bint Muʿawwidh says: "We used to go with the Prophet on his expeditions to give the people water and serve them. We also arranged the return of the wounded and the bodies of those who were killed to Madinah." (Related by al-Bukhari)

Umm ʿAṭiyyah, an Anṣārī companion of the Prophet, says: "I went with the Prophet on seven of his expeditions. I would stay behind with their equipment and cook for them." (Related by Muslim)

Cleaning Services

In Chapter Two, which discusses women's participation in social activities, we discuss the example of a woman who volunteered to clean the mosque. We have already mentioned the fact that a woman volunteering to provide a service does not mean that it must always be on a voluntary basis or that Islam does not permit it if compensation is provided for the same.

Domestic Work

In a report by Umm Salamah, the Prophet's wife, she says that she needed an explanation about a certain prayer: "... I sent him the maid and said to her: 'Stand by his side and say to him: Umm Salamah says: I had heard you telling people not to pray these two voluntary *rakʿahs* at this time, but I see you offering them now... The maid did just that...'" (Related by al-Bukhari and Muslim)

---

3. Al-Shifāʾ and Ḥafṣah belonged to the same clan of Quraysh.

Asmā' bint Abu Bakr reports: "When Al-Zubayr married me he had nothing in the world that he owned, neither money nor servant nor anything apart from a camel used to carry water and his horse. I used to feed his horse and fetch water. I also used to stitch the pail I used to bring the water and I made the dough for our bread... I also carried on my head the date stones from the plot of land the Prophet gave to al-Zubayr, which was about two miles away from our place... I continued to do so until Abu Bakr [my father] sent me a servant to look after the horse and its needs. It was like he freed me from bondage." (Related by al-Bukhari and Muslim)

Aspects Relating to Women's Professional Work in Modern Society

1. Modern education has advanced considerably, branching into a whole spectrum of areas and disciplines, and spanning several stages. Moreover, it is now provided for boys and girls. This enables women to undertake a wide variety of professions.
2. Medical care has also become varied, comprising different types and specialities that are provided to both men and women. Like education, medical care demonstrates society's need for women to undertake such professional work.
3. Fast travel, particularly air travel, necessitates the presence of hostesses to provide certain types of service to female passengers when needed.
4. Modern societies produce a wide range of products and clothing for women. This means that there is a need for women to work as shop assistants to serve customers, as also in purchasing and supplies.
5. The time gap between puberty and marriage has widened considerably as men take much longer these days before they are financially able to marry. This aspect of social life places young people under considerable strain and causes

much stress. Indeed, young people are often unable to get married and start a family unless both husband and wife go out to work.

6. Nowadays newly married couples prefer to live independently, whereas extended families, with several married sons and daughters, used to live together in one family home. This new phenomenon means that men need higher incomes in order to be able to establish a home for a fledgling family. It is often the case that this cannot be done without the wife's help. Moreover, social relations are now so complex that a woman's family are often unable to support her again, should she be divorced or should her husband die. She is often forced to work in order to earn her own living.
7. Wages in some Muslim societies have lagged behind while the cost of living has steadily risen. This has further emphasised the need for women to seek professional employment so as to help in establishing families.
8. Social development has led to the creation of large establishments controlling productivity in most industries and businesses, as well as in the provision of services including education and medicine. In times past most professions relied on individual efforts. Indeed, many services used to be provided from home, such as weaving, knitting, tailoring, food processing, dying, as well as teaching apprentices and other forms of education. Indeed, some types of medical treatment used to be provided from home. This radical social development has forced women to go out to work while in the past she could combine looking after her family with doing her professional work from home.
9. Despite women's roles and the fact that they remain responsible for the family home, society still needs an increasing number of them to undertake different types of employment. Yet the following considerations need to be taken into account:

- Many women can only work part time;
- Women need to take long leaves when they give birth to or look after new-born children;
- Some women find themselves forced to leave work altogether when they face special circumstances at home.

Islamic Principles Relevant to Women's Work in Our Times

Before looking at these Islamic principles we need to highlight two very important things: the various erroneous claims made by different people and the types of research needed to ensure that women's work is placed on a sound basis.

As regards the first point we need to explain that many claims made by different people concerning women's work and employment are totally wrong. Those who advocate a Western type of social change claim that married women must be financially and economically independent so that they can enjoy and exercise their free will. This, however, is a recipe for undermining the foundations of the family. To be of healthy and sound structure, the family must rely on the cooperation of its individual members and the proper division of responsibilities between them. It cannot be based on total independence of its members or on rivalry between them. Similarly, the claim that a woman cannot achieve personal fulfilment and develop her character unless she has a job is wrong. A woman can achieve such fulfilment and development when she is a housewife undertaking suitable measures for participation in social and political activity. Having said that, we do not deny that employment and professional work give a woman highly useful experience in life.

Likewise, those who take a hard line against women's work make false claims when they say that Islam prohibits such work by women except in situations of necessity. Thus they allege that such approval is based on the principle that 'Necessity relaxes restriction'. They also stress the complementary rule that 'Every necessity is dealt with on the basis of its actual impact'. To look at it in this way puts women's work on the same level as that of a starving person being allowed to eat what is forbidden in order to survive. We do not find any basis to the claim that women are not allowed to work. As for women's role at home, this is a social matter that can take a broad variety of forms according to her circumstances and social conditions. It is by no means subject to a definitive Islamic ruling.

As for the other point, women's professional work is a very serious and important development in our world, affecting many aspects of social and economic life, particularly within the family, the basic social unit. In order to put this development on its proper course so that it produces its highly beneficial effects and avoids negative aspects, it should be accompanied by proper development in the educational, social, economic and organisational fields. There is no denying, therefore, that social life has become extremely complex and all its aspects have mutual bearing on one another.

We pray and hope that scholars will undertake serious scientific studies in all relevant areas, starting with determining the essential differences between males and females, in all aspects of life and across different age groups. These studies should also address the system of education and the curricula suitable for boys and girls, as well as the sort of jobs suitable to both. Such studies form an essential basis for demarcating the line of development that should be followed in every field. With such studies and planning we hope that our society can have the necessary guidance and enlightenment for its development.

Principle One:

> Every woman should receive a proper standard of education that suits her, within a system of education that achieves the general objectives of Islamic education and fulfils two essential purposes: (1) enabling her to look after her family, home and children, giving them all the care they need, so as to live up to the hadith in which the Prophet says: "A woman is a shepherd in her husband's home and responsible for his family members and children;" and (2) giving her proper training in a profession that suits her. She can, thus, work when she has to meet personal, family or social needs.

Abu Burdah narrated from his father that the Prophet said: "Any man who has a young slave girl and he gives her proper education and initiates her in good manners, then sets her free and marries her shall have a double reward from God." (Related by al-Bukhari) If this applies to a slave girl and her education, educating one's own daughter carries greater importance.

'Ā'ishah narrated: "A woman with her two daughters came to me asking for help. I found nothing to give her except one date. I gave it to her and she divided it between her two daughters and went away. The Prophet came in later and I told him. He said: 'Whoever is responsible for girls and he takes good care of them, they will shield him from the Fire.'" (Related by al-Bukhari)

In his commentary on this hadith, Ibn Ḥajar quotes several hadiths relating to taking good care of girls. These hadiths have different chains of transmission. The hadiths include statements like: "... He supports them, provides for their marriages and teaches them good manners..." "... He treats them well and watches God in the way he brings them up..." and "... teaches them, treats them with compassion and looks after them..." Ibn Ḥajar adds: "All these qualities come under 'taking good care of them' which is the only aspect occurring in the hadith narrated by 'Ā'ishah."

Two points need to be made here. First, the hadith mentions the word *'iḥsān'* which means 'to be good to someone'. In our translation we used 'takes good care of girls'. The term used by the Prophet indicates that being good to a girl means providing her with the best chance to acquire proper moral values and a good education. While morality is constant, useful education varies in kind and standard from one generation or place to another. What is important is that it should give a girl what enables her to undertake her responsibilities well when she gets married.

Secondly, the woman mentioned in the hadith above would have been much kinder to her daughters while she herself would have been in a far better and more honourable position had she been able to work and look after herself and her daughters. To earn her living through some beneficial work is much better than depending on people's charity. Indeed, the Prophet describes charity as "no more than people's stain removers." (Related by Muslim)

The need to empower women so that they can work and earn a living is further emphasised in our time by the fact that most families would find it very difficult to look after an adult female again, should she be divorced or widowed, particularly if she has young children. Ibn 'Ābidīn, an eminent scholar says: "It is appropriate for a father to send his daughter to a woman who can teach her a skill such as embroidery or dress making," so as to be able to earn her living when the need arises. All this may be included under the general meaning of *iḥsān* which is mentioned in the hadith narrated by 'Ā'ishah.

In addition to basic general learning, the system of education for girls should, in our view, include three elements: (1) theoretical study of a suitable profession; (2) practical training in that profession.

Such training must be up to a good standard, so that if the girl gets married soon afterwards, without having had a chance to practise her profession, she can restart when necessary, taking some fresh training to enable her to work, and (3) a study of the general Islamic principles concerning women's professional work.

Principle Two:

> Every woman should be able to utilise her time fully, so as to be a useful and productive member of her community. She must never be satisfied with being idle at any stage of life, during her youth, maturity or old age, whether she is a daughter or wife, divorced or widowed. Should she have spare time, she should use it in some suitable and beneficial work.

God says in the Qur'an: "Whoever does righteous deeds, whether man or woman, and is a believer, We shall most certainly give a good life. And We shall indeed reward these according to the best that they ever did." (16: 97) This verse sums up the principle that men and women are rewarded for their good deeds. A hadith by the Prophet highlights the importance of putting our time to good use, giving a strong warning against wasting time in anything other than such good pursuit. It shows us that we will be accountable for the use of every minute of our lives just as we are to account for every little action we do, whether good or bad. Abu Barzah quotes the Prophet as saying: "No one will be able to move [on the Day of Judgement] before he is questioned about his life and what he did during it, his knowledge and how he utilised it, his money and how he earned and spent it, and his body and to what use he put it." (Related by al-Tirmidhi)

Principle Three:

> It is obligatory for a husband to support his wife so that she does not need to work for a living. A father is responsible

for supporting his daughter in the same way. Should a man be incapable of discharging this duty or should he die without leaving enough for his women to live on, the state takes over this responsibility.

1. A husband's responsibility:

God says in the Qur'an: "Men shall take full care of women with the bounties with which God has favoured some of them more abundantly than others and with what they may spend of their own wealth." (4: 34) Jābir ibn ʿAbdullāh quotes the Prophet as saying: "... You owe to them [i.e. your wives] that you should look after them and provide them with clothes in a reasonable manner..." (Related by Muslim) ʿĀ'ishah narrates that "Hind bint ʿUtbah said to the Prophet: 'Messenger of God! Abu Sufyān [her husband] is stingy. He does not give me enough to look after myself and my children, unless I take from him without his knowledge.' He said to her: 'Take what is sufficient for you and your children in a reasonable manner.'" (Related by al-Bukhari and Muslim)

2. A father's responsibility:

Abu Hurayrah quotes the Prophet as saying: "... Begin with your dependents. A woman may say, 'You either provide me with food, or else divorce me'... And a son may say, 'Provide me with food. To whom are you leaving me?'" (Related by al-Bukhari) Ibn Ḥajar says that the Prophet's statement, "Provide me with food. To whom are you leaving me?" has been taken to mean that if a child has money or a trade, then the father is not required to support that child. The one who wonders to whom it is being left must be one who has no means of its own other than its father's support. A person who has money or a trade does not fall into this category. Al-Khayyir al-Ramlī says: "If a woman has sufficient means, having a trade like dress-making or weaving, she should pay for her living."

3. The state's responsibility:

   Abu Hurayrah quotes the Prophet as saying: "I have more claim on the believers than they have on their own selves. Therefore, if any believer leaves an outstanding debt, I will settle it, and whoever of them leaves any property, it goes to his heirs." In another version, the Prophet says: "Whoever leaves behind any dependents, then such dependents are in our care." (Related by al-Bukhari) Ibn Ḥajar comments: "By including this hadith under the headings of 'liabilities', al-Bukhari signifies that if a believer dies, leaving behind young children with no means of support, then they are entitled to support from the Muslim state."

   'Abdullāh ibn 'Umar quotes the Prophet as saying: "Every one of you is a shepherd and accountable for those under his care. The ruler is a shepherd and he is responsible for his subjects." (Related by al-Bukhari and Muslim)

   Zayd ibn Aslam narrated from his father: "I went out to the market place with 'Umar ibn al-Khaṭṭāb and a young woman caught up with 'Umar. She said to him: 'My husband has died leaving behind young children. By God they do not have the means to feed themselves, and they have neither a land to till nor cattle.' 'Umar stopped with her for a while... He then went home where he had tied a strong camel. He placed on the camel two sacks which he filled with food and put in between them some money and clothing. He gave the camel's rein to the woman saying: 'Lead him away. You will not have used this up before God brings you something good...'" (Related by al-Bukhari)

Principle Four:

> The man is responsible for the family. Therefore, a wife or a daughter should seek his permission before taking up employment. God says in the Qur'an: "Men shall take full care of women." (4: 34)

'Abdullāh ibn 'Umar quotes the Prophet as saying: "... A man is a shepherd of his family and he is responsible for them..." (Related by al-Bukhari) Needless to say, man's headship of the family and his authority within it is governed by Islamic rules and the traditions of society. Hence, he cannot use it arbitrarily to prevent his wife or daughter from doing a job that is of benefit to her or to society without a very good reason. Nor is it right that he should force either to unnecessarily take up a job.

Principle Five:

> It is recommended, or sometimes obligatory, for a Muslim woman to get married at an early age so that she preserves her chastity and contributes to the preservation of her society where men and women enjoy a high standard of psychological well-being and proper morality. Sometimes, it is strongly discouraged or even forbidden for her to work if such work prevents her from marrying or unnecessarily delays her marriage. On the other hand, she is strongly recommended to work if such work facilitates her marriage.

Anas ibn Mālik quotes the Prophet as saying: "... By God, I am the most God-fearing among you but I fast at times and do not fast at others; I pray at night and I go to sleep; and I marry women. Whoever wilfully declines to follow my way does not belong to me." (Related by al-Bukhari and Muslim)

‘Abdullāh ibn Mas‘ūd narrated: “We were with the Prophet, a group of young men and we had nothing. He said to us: ‘You, young men! Whoever of you can afford marriage should get married. It helps you to lower your gaze and maintain your chastity.’” (Related by al-Bukhari)

For women, marriage is either encouraged or a duty. Therefore, if taking up a job without real need for it means that she will not marry, then taking such work becomes either discouraged or forbidden.

‘Urwah ibn al-Zubayr says that he asked his aunt, ‘Ā’ishah, about the meaning of the Qur’anic verse that says, “If you fear that you may not deal fairly by the orphans, you may marry of other women as may be agreeable to you.” (4: 3) She said: “My nephew! This verse refers to an orphan girl brought up by a guardian who may admire her beauty or wants her for her money but wishes to give her a small dowry. Men are commanded not to marry such girls unless they give them their full dowry. They are ordered to marry other women instead.” (Related by al-Bukhari) In both the Qur’anic verse and the hadith orphan girls are mentioned. Yet this serves as an indication that it is preferable to provide girls with husbands at an early age. Scholars differ as to whether this means after they attain puberty or even before it. The weightier view is that it means after attaining puberty. The Prophet encouraged early marriage for girls to discourage immorality and to ensure chastity and sound mental health. He said: “Had Usāmah been a girl, I would have dressed her well and made her look attractive so as to get her married.” This is why we say that early marriage is recommended. Delaying marriage because of a woman’s job is certainly discouraged. However, it is important to clarify that the concept of early marriage differs from one generation and social environment to another. In the past, early marriage meant shortly after puberty. In our modern times, it is several years later, and the number of years differs between rural and urban areas.

As marriage is closely related to a natural human need, Islam attaches to it many aspects of care so as to facilitate it. These include a man being able to approach other good people so as to arrange the marriage of his daughter or sister to someone suitable; a woman proposing marriage to a good man; accepting a very small dowry that may be no more than a ring made of iron or teaching the prospective wife a few Qur'anic surahs. All these and similar ones, will be discussed with relevant texts in the section on the family.

It is in line with the Islamic principle that encourages and facilitates marriage that we have argued that women are encouraged to take up employment or professional jobs if this facilitates marriage. This certainly applies when most men who want to get married are unable to earn enough to look after a family. Indeed, the question of *women* taking up employment becomes a duty, rather than merely encouraged, if a family is certain that having a job is necessary for their daughter to get married. A major rule of Islamic law says: "What is indispensable for the fulfilment of a duty is itself a duty." Scholars emphasise their view that marriage is a duty incumbent on any person, man or woman, whose chastity is unlikely to be maintained without it. This applies in even larger measure today given the widespread means of temptation and seduction.

Principle Six:

> Muslim woman are keen to have children within the means of her family and the needs of her society. It is unacceptable that her job should deprive her of this.

God says in the Qur'an: "God has given you spouses of your own kind and has given you, through your spouses, children and grand-children." (16: 72) Jābir mentions that the Prophet said to him: "Jābir! Try to have what is good for you." (Related by al-Bukhari and Muslim) Commenting on this hadith, Ibn Ḥajar mentions in his book, *Fatḥ al-Bārī*: "'Iyāḍ says that al-Bukhari and other scholars explain the phrase 'what is good for you' mentioned in the hadith as meaning 'to seek to have children'. This is certainly true." Ibn Ḥajar goes on to explain the derivation of the Arabic term *kays* used by the Prophet. Indeed the Prophet urges us all to try to have children. He says: "Marry women who are caring, loving and child bearing. I will take pride in your numbers." (Related by al-Nasā'ī)

Principle Seven:

> Every woman is duty-bound to look after her home and her children as best she can. Her job or professional work must not obstruct her fulfilment of this duty, which must remain the primary responsibility of married women.

In the Qur'an, God says: "Among His signs is that He creates for you spouses out of your own kind, so that you might incline towards them, and He engenders love and tenderness between you." (30: 21) 'Abdullāh ibn 'Umar mentions that the Prophet said: "... A woman is a shepherd of her husband's home and children, and she is responsible for them." (Related by al-Bukhari and Muslim) Abu Hurayrah quotes the Prophet as saying: "The best women to ride camels are the good ones among the Quraysh women: they are the most caring of children when they are young and the most considerate of husbands regarding their money." (Related by al-Bukhari)

Every man, woman and child is fully entitled to live in a happy home where they find happiness, love and a mutually caring atmosphere. The man needs to find full comfort at home, which is best provided by a loving and caring wife. It is to this that the Qur'anic verse refers: "He creates for you spouses... so that you might incline towards them." He also finds happiness in playing with his young children. Needless to say, when a man finds comfort and renewed strength, his output is increased in quantity and quality, whatever the nature of his work may be.

Even though a woman may have a professional job, her home remains her little haven where she finds comfort and happiness. It is there that she feels her husband's caring attitude and enjoys her children's love. She is, thus, able to give more to her family and her job, and to improve the quality of what she gives.

Children need proper family care throughout the various stages of growing up. This includes being breast-fed by their mothers and being fully cared for by her, rather than anyone else, for at least three years, except perhaps in extremely exceptional circumstances. Children also need wise and caring upbringing by both parents until they attain a stage of maturity. All this should be provided in an atmosphere of love and tenderness, together with attention to religious duties. When all this is fulfilled, the home becomes a true haven for husband, wife and children. In such a happy haven, the young buds will open up, the little flowers will blossom, and the roses will spread their fine scent when the woman looks after it with her heart and mind. Therefore, when a woman pursues her career, she must always look for proper balance between her commitments. She must not allow her career to jeopardize her responsibilities at home. Her success in her profession must never be allowed to disturb the proper balance, leaving her too preoccupied with the superficial attractions of her career to attend to her more important role at home.

Principle Eight:

> A woman must pursue a career in two situations: (1) if she needs to earn her own living or her family's living because she has no one else to fulfil that responsibility; and (2) if she is needed as part of a female collective duty providing something that the Muslim community requires. However, she must try her best to achieve a balance between undertaking such an incumbent duty and fulfilling her family responsibilities.

1. A WOMAN'S NEED TO EARN HER LIVING:

Jābir ibn ʿAbdullāh reports: "My aunt was divorced. She wanted to go and gather her dates. A man reproached her for wanting to go out. She went to the Prophet and told him. He said to her: 'Yes, you can gather your fruit. It may be that you will give something for charity, or do some other good work.'" (Related by Muslim)

ʿĀ'ishah narrated: "A woman with her two daughters came to me asking for help. I found nothing to give her except for one date. I gave it to her and she divided it between her two daughters and went away." (Related by al-Bukhari)

Perhaps it is useful to repeat here what we said under Principle One above: The woman mentioned in the second of these two hadiths would have been much kinder to her daughters while she herself would have been in a far better and more honourable position had she been able to work and look after herself and her daughters. To earn her living through some beneficial work is much better than depending on people's charity. Indeed the Prophet describes charity as "No more than people's stain removers. " (Related by Muslim)

Ibn al-Qayyim says: "Scholars differ on whether a wife whose husband cannot provide for her living can apply for the annulment of her marriage. Al-Shāfiʿī gives two views... The second view is that she cannot make such an application but the husband must not stand in her way if she seeks a job and earns her own living... Abu Ḥanīfah and his two disciples express this same view. A totally different point of view is that the woman is required to support him if he is unable to support himself. This is the view expressed by Ibn Ḥazm who says in *al-Muḥallā*: 'If the husband is unable to support himself and his wife is rich, she is assigned a duty to support him. She cannot claim a refund of anything she spends on him should he subsequently become well off.' Scholars also say that God has commanded a creditor to give his debtor more time to settle his debt if he is in difficult circumstances. God also recommended the creditor to forego his claim as an act of charity. Anything other than these two options is unfair and disallowed in Islam. We say to such a woman the same as God said: either delay your claim until such a time when he is able to fulfil his obligation or forego your right as an act of charity. Other than these two options you have no right."

In my view, there is no difference between the situation of a woman who is rich as a result of inheritance and one who has a job that makes her well off. Blessed be her earnings if she uses them to provide her family with a good living.

2. Society's need of what can be considered a collective duty:

In relation to those who are required to fulfil them, duties are divided into personal and collective. A personal duty is required of every one of those to whom Islamic duties apply. Everyone must personally fulfil such a duty; no one can undertake its fulfilment on behalf of someone else. Examples of such personal duties are prayers, fasting, zakat, pilgrimage, fulfilment of contracts, refraining from drinking and gambling, etc. A collective duty denotes something that God requires of the whole community of His servants, but not on an individual basis. Thus, if a number of them undertake it, the duty of the community is deemed to have been fulfilled. Those who do not take part in its fulfilment are not accountable for any negligence. If no one undertakes this duty, then the whole community is accountable for the omission. Examples of collective duties are enjoining what is right and beneficial, forbidding what is wrong and harmful, offering the Funeral, i.e. *Janāzah*, Prayer for the deceased, building hospitals, saving a drowning person, putting out a fire, learning medicine and other specialised professions the community needs, administering justice, issuing Islamic rulings on matters facing people, answering greetings and giving a testimony when one is called as a witness. In all such matters, God, the Lawgiver, requires that the community fulfils them, no matter who actually undertakes the task. He does not require every individual to undertake the fulfilment of every such duty. The community's interests are served when some people fulfil these duties.

Thus, the whole community must ensure that a collective duty is fulfilled. A person who is able to undertake it by his efforts or money must do so, while one who does not have such ability must encourage the one who is able and even pressurise him into doing it if he is reluctant to do so. When the duty is discharged, they have all discharged their responsibilities. If they neglect it, they all incur a sin: the one who is able incurs the sin of failing to do it, and the one who does not have such ability incurs the sin of failing to encourage and pressurise the other to do it. Thus, the whole community is jointly and severally responsible for the fulfilment of such duties.

To give an example: if a group of people see a person about to drown and some of them are good swimmers and are skilled in saving a drowning person while the others do not swim, it is a duty of the first group that some of them should do their best to save that person. If they fail to rush to his rescue, the others must urge them to do so. Once the purpose has been fulfilled, they are all deemed to have discharged their duty. If the purpose remains unfulfilled, they all incur a sin. Should only one person in the community be able to fulfil a collective duty, it becomes a personal duty for that person. Thus, in our example if only one person is a good swimmer and skilled in saving a drowning person, he must do so. If an accident is witnessed by one person and he is called to testify, giving such testimony is obligatory on him. If there is only one doctor in the community and he is assigned the task of attending to casualties, this becomes his personal duty.

Collective duties on women, with regard to professional work, are those that the needs of the Muslim community require of women generally. These are, in fact, social necessities. They may be tasks that only women can fulfil or they may require the participation of women. On the other hand, they may be tasks for men but the community lacks such efforts and needs women to provide them. Examples of these are teaching, nursing and providing medical care for women, taking custody of young children, teaching children, looking after orphans, taking care of young delinquents, as well as certain areas of social work, etc.

Imam al-Ḥaramayn al-Juwaynī succinctly highlights the importance of discharging collective duties: "To discharge a collective duty earns greater reward than the fulfilment of a personal duty. If a man neglects a personal duty, he alone bears the sin involved in such omission. Likewise, if he fulfils it, the reward is his own. Suppose that a collective duty remains unfulfilled, a sin is incurred by all in the community, with varying degrees according to their positions and abilities. Therefore, the one who fulfils such a duty removes the liability of punishment from himself and all others, and looks for earning the best reward. We cannot underrate the action of one who acts for the entire Muslim community in the fulfilment of a religious duty. Besides, what is considered a collective duty may become a personal one for particular people."

Principle Nine:

> A Muslim woman is encouraged to pursue a career, providing it does not lead to negligence of her family responsibilities, for any of the following purposes: 1) providing help to her poor husband, father or brother;[4] 2) ensuring a real interest of the Muslim community; and 3) using some of her earnings in good and beneficial ways.

---

4. Needless to say, helping female relatives falls within the same category, if not taking priority.

1. Help a poor relative

Zaynab, ʿAbdullāh ibn Masʿūd's wife, reports: "... As we stood there, Bilāl came over. We said to him: Ask the Prophet for us if it is acceptable that I pay out my charity as part of what I spend on my husband and the orphans I am looking after. We told him not to tell the Prophet who we were. Bilāl went in and put our question to the Prophet. The Prophet asked him who we were. Bilāl said: 'Zaynab.' The Prophet asked: 'Which Zaynab?' He said: 'ʿAbdullāh's wife.' The Prophet said: 'Yes it does. She indeed earns two rewards: one for doing a kindness to relatives and one for her charity.'" In another version, the Prophet is quoted as saying to her: "Your husband and your children are the ones who most deserve your charity." (Related by al-Bukhari and Muslim)

Ibn Ḥajar writes in his voluminous work *Fatḥ al-Bārī* in which he explains every hadith in al-Bukhari's *Ṣaḥīḥ* anthology of authentic hadiths: "Many scholars understand the term 'charity' in the hadith to refer to the obligatory one, i.e. zakat. Their basis is the way Zaynab phrased her question, saying: 'if it is acceptable...'. This view is emphatically confirmed by al-Mazarī. ʿIyāḍ objects saying that in urging women to be charitable, the Prophet told them that they should give to charity, 'even from your jewellery'. Coupled with the fact that Zaynab was a skilled woman who made things and sold them, this confirms that her charity was a voluntary one. This view is strongly supported by al-Nawawī. Scholars who share this second view interpret her question, 'is it acceptable...', to mean would it be enough as a shield for her from hell. She feared that if she paid her voluntary charity to her husband and her relative orphans, she would not receive the reward she hoped for. His reference to her having skills is cited by al-Ṭaḥāwī in support of Abu Ḥanīfah's view confirming that she earned through her skills what she spent on her husband and children, saying that this indicates that her charity was of the voluntary type."

We may add that when a woman pursues a career or utilises her skills to earn money to provide her family with a decent standard of living, she does extremely well.

2. Ensure a real interest of the Muslim community

Some women are gifted in different ways. Some are talented in the way they express ideas or how they talk to people and influence them. Some excel in poetry and other forms of literature, using their gifts to produce a good effect on people. Others have the intelligence to learn and innovate. Such women should receive proper care so that their gifts can develop and flourish. We should always remember that such women may achieve a higher degree of excellence in their specialities than many men.

3. Use earnings in good and beneficial ways.

ʿĀ'ishah narrated: "... The one with the longest hand among us was Zaynab, because she used to work in some handicraft and gave to charity some of what she earned." (Related by Muslim)

ʿĀ'ishah said: "... I have never seen a woman who is better in faith or more God-fearing or truthful in what she says or kind to relatives or charitable or more modest in her work through which she earns what she gives for charity, purely to please God, than Zaynab [bint Jaḥsh]." (Related by Muslim)

Jābir ibn ʿAbdullāh reports: "My aunt was divorced. She wanted to go and gather her dates. A man reproached her for wanting to go out. She went to the Prophet and told him. He said to her: 'Yes, you can gather your fruit. It may be that you will give something for charity or do some other good work.'" (Related by Muslim)

Principle Ten:

> Every man is strongly recommended to help his wife in her household work when her job leaves little time for her to do so. He is duty bound to help her if the work she does is in fulfilment of a duty.

'Abdullāh ibn 'Umar quotes the Prophet as saying: "A man is a shepherd looking after members of his household and he is accountable for this." (Related by al-Bukhari and Muslim)

Al-Aswad ibn Yazīd mentions that he asked 'Ā'ishah: "What did the Prophet do at home?" She said: "He would attend to the needs of his family. When he heard the call to prayer, he would leave home." (Related by al-Bukhari) May God shower His mercy on al-Bukhari, for his scholarly insight manifested itself best in his subheadings which he chose for the different sections in his anthology of authentic hadiths. He included this hadith under different subheadings, which were: 'Man's service to his family', 'Anyone serving his family' and 'How a man should behave when he is with his family'.

One way that ensures that a man fulfils his responsibilities of taking good care of his family is that he should generally help his wife in looking after their home and children. Giving such help becomes even more pressing when she has to fulfil the duties of her own job. Indeed, when a man helps his wife domestically, a fairer sharing of responsibilities inside and outside the home is ensured. Moreover, it nurtures feelings of mutual love and compassion between man and wife. The Prophet used to milk his sheep and attend to his own needs as well as mend his robes, repair his shoes and do all that men do at home. (Related by Ahmad) He did all this despite the fact that his wives had only their domestic duties to attend to. What then is to be expected from a Muslim whose wife has a full time job? Three verses of the Qur'an emphasise a man's duty to help his wife. These are: "Help one another in furthering righteousness and piety." (5: 2)

"Women shall, in all fairness, enjoy rights similar to those exercised against them." (2: 228) "God does not charge a soul with more than it can bear." (2: 286)

Principle Eleven:

> When a woman takes up a job, the couple should agree on a reasonable way of using the woman's income from that job.

Kurayb, Ibn 'Abbās's *mawlā*, mentions, "Maymūnah bint al-Ḥārith, the Prophet's wife, told him that she set free a slave woman she had, without mentioning this first to the Prophet. When it was her day, she said to him: 'Messenger of God! Have you noticed that I set my slave woman free?' He said: 'Have you done that?' She confirmed that she did. He said: 'Had you given her to your maternal uncles, you could have earned greater reward.'" (Related by al-Bukhari and Muslim)

Zaynab, 'Abdullāh ibn Mas'ūd's wife, reports: "... As we stood there, Bilāl came over. We said to him: Ask the Prophet for me if it is acceptable that I pay out my charity as part of what I spend on my husband and the orphans I am looking after ... The Prophet said: 'Yes it does. She indeed earns two rewards: one for doing a kindness to relatives and one for her charity.'" (Related by al-Bukhari and Muslim)

Mutual agreement between a married couple on all their affairs is the preferred way of doing things. It is indeed the proper way for a family life based on mutual love and tenderness and sharing together all that life brings. The question is what is to be done if such mutual agreement on the use of a woman's income is not achieved? The hadith quoting Maymūnah suggests that a woman is completely free to use her money as she thinks fit, but it also indicates that it is preferable for her to consult her husband. We will discuss the mutual financial claims of husband and wife in the section devoted to the family.

The second hadith, reported by Zaynab, includes a recommendation that a woman should help her husband financially. However, the very fact that a woman goes out to work, particularly in present day conditions, presents certain physical and mental difficulties for her husband, which he would not have had if her time was fully devoted to her household duties. From the Islamic point of view, a man is entitled to her attention to her family duties, as he alone is responsible for paying all his family's needs. Therefore, a portion of the income from the woman's work should compensate him for those difficulties. The determination of such compensation should be the subject of a ruling issued by a proper religious authority so that every couple can make an informed decision. We will here only present a suggestion for study:

1. All normal expenses of the family are borne by the husband, as financial responsibility is assigned to him in the first place;
2. The wife pays for any additional expenses the family incurs as a result of her taking up her job;
3. The wife gives her husband a portion of her income in compensation for the difficulties he has to bear in consequence of her work. This portion differs according to the financial circumstances of each of the married couple. The one who is well off should forego their claims so as to enable the other party to give more to charity and contribute to good causes. The best option, however, is to determine the matter through the mutual love and tenderness a couple should nurture.

Principle Twelve:

The Muslim community shares a responsibility in facilitating the means that help working women discharge their domestic and professional duties. God says: "The believers, men and women, are friends of one another." (9: 71)

Al-Nu'mān ibn Bashīr quotes the Prophet as saying: "In their mutual compassion, love and tenderness, the believers are like one body: when any organ suffers a complaint, the whole body is afflicted with sleeplessness and fever." (Related by al-Bukhari and Muslim)

Everyone in the Muslim community as well as all its institutions and distinguished figures exercise such mutual compassion and tenderness. It is important, therefore, that people of influence should join efforts to overcome the difficulties a woman faces as a result of having to combine taking up a job and attending to her household and family duties. Such efforts may include:

- The establishment of good quality nurseries for young children in every quarter, and in major companies and establishments;
- Encouraging initiatives that enable women to do their professional work from home;
- Providing the facilities that help more women to work from home if such facilities require collective rather than individual resources. To give some examples:
    - Women may take part in home productivity, whether this is limited to domestic industries or includes some sophisticated industries where different parts are produced in the workers' homes before they are sent to factories for assembly. We may add here that different initiatives in this area have proven to be very successful. Indeed, a considerable portion of exports in some countries rely on such domestic production.
    - Women can undertake certain services that they are able to do at home such as preparing ready or almost ready meals and using a home where the family has only one child as a nursery for a small number of children.

Principle Thirteen:

> In a Muslim state, the government is responsible for two essential matters in respect of working women: 1) to ensure that a married man who is a government employee receives a suitable salary to enable him to provide for his family's needs with no need for his wife to take a job; and 2) to provide suitable conditions for women who are government employees.

'Abdullāh ibn 'Umar quotes the Prophet as saying: "Every one of you is a shepherd and you are all accountable for your folks: a ruler who is in charge of people is a shepherd and is accountable for them..." (Related by al-Bukhari and Muslim)

Here are some examples of the duties a Muslim government should fulfil to help working women:

1. Take into full consideration the special characteristics of both men and women in all government departments that employ both sexes. It is important that this should rely on comprehensive psychological and social studies.
2. Attaching children's nurseries to government offices enables working women to provide necessary childcare during allowed breaks. Sufficient nurseries should also be established in residential areas.
3. Providing the means and facilities that help people to observe the values of Islamic morality in mixed situations, whether at the place of work or on means of transport.
4. Enacting regulations that enable women to combine their family duties and their work, such as giving long maternity and childcare leaves. Such leave may be on full or half pay and may extend up to three years. Such regulations may also allow an employed mother who needs to look after young children to work part time, on full or half pay. Women's

working hours may also be looked into so as to give them shorter attendance at work. This may also give the added advantage of reducing overcrowding on public transport and reducing traffic congestion during rush hour.

Principle Fourteen:

> Women should not undertake jobs that are unsuited to their nature or physical and psychological characteristics. Such jobs are of two types: 1) a type Islam specifically and categorically prohibits; and 2) a type determined by the Muslim community.

1. What Islam prohibits

Abu Bakrah quotes the Prophet as saying: "A community that assigns its affairs to a woman shall not prosper." (Related by al-Bukhari)

Commenting on this hadith, Professor Muṣṭafā al-Sibāʿī says:

> This applies to the post of overall ruler. The Prophet said it when he received the news that the Persians appointed one of their deceased emperor's daughters to succeed him. Moreover, there is no blanket prohibition that excludes women from being in charge of others. This is universally agreed upon by all scholars. Indeed, all leading scholars, without exception, agree that a woman may be in charge of children and mentally retarded adults, act for a group of people in managing their business or farms, as also act as a witness in legal cases. To act as a witness is, according to scholars, a form of *walāyah*, which is the term used by the Prophet in referring to the assignment of affairs in the above-quoted hadith. Moreover, Abu Ḥanīfah considers that a woman is entitled to hold the post of judge, which is certainly a form of *walāyah*, and a position of great responsibility. Thus the hadith should be

> understood as a prohibition of assigning the post of head of state, or a post of similar responsibility, to a woman... All other jobs may be assigned to women, provided that this is done in accordance with Islamic principles and values.[5]

Ibn Rushd, or Averroes as he is known in European cultures, says in reference to women being appointed as judges:

> Scholars differ on whether a judge must be male. The majority make this a condition for a judgement to be valid. Abu Ḥanīfah says that a woman can be a judge in commercial and financial disputes. Al-Ṭabarī, on the other hand, considers it permissible that a woman can judge in all affairs... Thus, scholars who exclude women from judicial posts take such posts to be like that of a head of state... Those who accept that she judges commercial and financial disputes consider this as an extension to the fact that she may give evidence as a witness in such disputes. Those who accept that women can judge all cases maintain that whoever can arbitrate between people may be given a post of judge, except for the universally agreed restriction that excludes women from the post of head of state.[6]

2. What the Muslim community determines

These may include any work that is physically and consistently very demanding, or mentally stressful, or requires a tough and hard attitude that women generally find too onerous.

We would like to quote here a view expressed by Shaykh Muhammad al-Ghazali on the type of government posts a woman may assume

5. Muṣṭafā al-Sibāʿī, *Al-Mar'ah bayn al-Fiqh wal-Qānūn*, "Women in Islamic Jurisprudence and Law" pp. 39–40, and 167. – Author's note.
6. Ibn Rushd, *Bidāyat al-Mujtahid*, Vol. 2, p. 344. – Author's note.

in our modern times. We feel that his view should be carefully considered and debated by the highly qualified among our contemporary scholars.

The main principles that should govern relations between the two sexes are outlined in the following Qur'anic and hadith statements: "Their Lord answers them: I will not suffer the work of any worker among you, male or female, to be lost." (3: 195) "Whoever does righteous deeds, whether man or woman, and is a believer, We shall most certainly give a good life. And We shall indeed reward these according to the best that they ever did." (16: 97) The Prophet says: "Women are full sisters of men." There are certain things which are not subject to any religious order or prohibition. These are thus left for us to determine according to what we see fit. No one may suggest that their views on such matters are part of our religion. These are merely their own views. This is perhaps the basis of Ibn Ḥazm's view that Islam has not restricted women from assuming any post other than that of head of an Islamic state.

I have heard someone rejecting Ibn Ḥazm's views, claiming that it is in conflict with the Qur'anic statement: "Men shall take full care of women with the bounties with which God has favoured some of them more abundantly than others, and with what they may spend of their own wealth." (4: 34) The person concerned understands this verse as restricting women from being the boss of any man in any type of job. This is totally wrong. Whoever reads the complete verse realizes that it speaks of a man's responsibility at home and within his own family. 'Umar appointed al-Shifā' as controller of the market in Madinah, giving her full powers over all those trading in the market, whether men or women. Her duties were thus: to allow what Islam permits, prevent what Islam prohibits, ensure justice and outlaw all offences. A man who is married to a doctor working in a hospital cannot intervene in her professional work.

It may be said that Ibn Ḥazm's view contradicts the hadith that says: "A community that assigns its affairs to a woman shall not prosper." Hence, assigning the affairs of Muslims to women is bound to lead to the failure of the Muslim community. Therefore, no post should be assigned to women, whether major or minor. Ibn Ḥazm maintains that the hadith speaks only of the post of overall ruler. It does not refer to any lesser post. We need to look at the hadith more carefully, but let us make clear that we are not advocating that women should be heads of state or prime ministers. What we strongly advocate is that the best qualified person should be the one who is made head of state or prime minister.

I have reflected on this hadith, which is authentic and correct, to establish its meaning. The Persian Empire had started to retreat in the face of the Islamic advance. It was run by an ill-fated, tyrannical royal family that left no room for consultation and allowed no dissent. Its religion was idolatrous. Relations between people in the community were very poor. A man might kill his father or brother for personal gain. The people were submissive. As the army suffered defeats and the Empire began to lose some of its territories, it perhaps would have been wiser to assign the task to an experienced military leader who could take measures to check the retreat. However, political idolatry left the empire in the hands of a girl who was totally unqualified. This was a signal that the whole empire was on the verge of collapse. When the Prophet was informed of this fact, he made his absolutely true statement, commenting on the state of affairs in that empire. Had the Persian Empire been run by a consultative government and the woman in charge was similar in experience and qualification to Golda Meir, the Jewish woman who ruled Israel, leaving the military strategy to be mapped by military commanders, such conditions would have merited a totally different comment.

Some clarification may be needed here. The Prophet read out Surah 27, The Ant, to people in Makkah. The surah gives a detailed account of the Queen of Sheba, a truly wise and intelligent woman who led her people to faith and success. The Prophet would never make a comment establishing a rule that contradicts revelations he received from on High. The Queen of Sheba ruled over a vast kingdom. The hoopoe who brought information about her to the Prophet Solomon described her and her community in the following Qur'anic verse: "I found there a woman ruling over them; and she has been given of all good things, and hers is a magnificent throne." (27: 23) Prophet Solomon called on her to believe and declare her submission to God, counselling her against taking a stubborn, arrogant attitude. When she received his letter, she felt that she should consider matters carefully before sending a reply. She consulted her advisers who were quick to declare their support of any decision she made. They declared: "We are endowed with power and with mighty prowess in war; but the command is yours. Consider, then, what you would command." (27: 33)

A woman of profound insight as she was, she did not let her people's ready obedience or her military power obscure her judgement. She decided to test Solomon so that she could establish whether he was a power hungry ruler who sought to extend his kingdom or a prophet advocating a true faith. When she met him, she used all her undoubted intelligence to make an enlightened judgement of him. She studied all that she saw of his affairs and how he ran his kingdom. It was soon clear to her that he was truly a prophet of God. She remembered the letter he had first sent to her which she had described to her advisers in the following words, reported in the Qur'an: "It is from Solomon, and it reads: In the name of God, the Lord of Grace, the Ever Merciful: Do not exalt yourselves against me, but come to me in submission [to God]." (27: 30–31) She, thus, came to her wise decision to discard her idolatrous religion and embrace the divine faith. "She said: My Lord! I have indeed wronged my soul, but now I submit myself, with Solomon, to God, the Lord of all the worlds." (27: 44) Can it ever be said that a community who had assigned its affairs to such a magnificent woman ended in failure? She was far more honourable than the man to whom the Thamūd assigned the task of killing the she-camel in disobedience of the Prophet Ṣāliḥ: "They called their friend, who took something and slew her. How grievous was My punishment and how true were My warnings. We sent against them a single blast, and they became like the dry twigs of the sheepfold builder. We have made the Qur'an easy to bear in mind: will anyone take heed?" (54: 29–32)

Once more I confirm that I have no special preference to assigning positions of great responsibilities to women. Few are the women who are greatly talented and they are often identified by coincidence. All I am trying to do is to explain a hadith that is entered in hadith anthologies and to show that there is no contradiction between it and the facts of history. The golden age of the British Empire occurred during the reign of Queen Victoria. Today, Britain's leadership is in the hands of a queen and a woman female Prime Minister.[7]

7. Shaikh Muhammad al-Ghazali wrote this when Margaret Thatcher was Britain's Prime Minister.

Nevertheless, it is going through a period of outstanding economic prosperity and political stability. How could it be said that the British people who assigned their leadership to these women did not prosper?

I wrote elsewhere about the crushing blows that were levelled at the Muslim people in the Indian subcontinent at the hands of Indira Gandhi. She was able to split the Muslim country of that subcontinent into two, and she thus achieved the ambitions of her people. It was Marshal Yahya Khan who, by contrast, ended in miserable failure. The catastrophes that befell the Arab countries when Golda Meir led Israel are countless. To undo their effect may require the full efforts of a whole generation. The question is not one of male and female. It is a question of moral values, personal qualities and talents. Indira Gandhi subsequently called general elections and was defeated. Later on, her people returned her to office in another free election.

Which of the two parties deserves to receive God's help and assume leadership on earth? Why do we not remember Ibn Taymiyyah's words: "God may support an unbeliever state, if it maintains justice, against a Muslim state which allows injustice to spread."

What importance does maleness have? A religious woman enjoying strong support among her people is much better than a long-bearded unbeliever.[8]

Having quoted Shaikh Muhammad al-Ghazali's view on this very serious matter, it is important to remind readers of another of his

8. Muhammad al-Ghazali, *al-Sunnah al-Nabawiyyah Bayn Ahl al-Fiqh wa Ahl al-Hadith*, pp. 47–51. – Author's note.

statements: "God knows that as much as I value my independence, I strongly dislike disputes and dissent. I prefer to be with the community. I am always ready to discard my own views in order to maintain the unity of the Muslim community."[9]

Principle Fifteen:

> When women's work necessitates mixing with men, both men and women must observe the Islamic manners and values which we have discussed in details elsewhere in this book. These include observing the Islamic dress code, lowering one's gaze, avoiding situations where one man is alone with one woman and congested situations. Likewise, situations where the same men and women are repeatedly together for long hours, as happens when men and women are together throughout the working day, even though each is doing their own job, must be avoided. Where the nature of work makes such repeated mixing unavoidable, because inputs by all are needed, a measured exception is granted.

It may be said that some institutions do not pay proper attention to Islamic manners and values. Should we in such cases forego the certain interests of working women or the Muslim community and prevent women from working there? Or is it better to give preference to these interests while we exert efforts to ensure that Islamic values are duly observed?

The rules Islam lays down require that needs and interests are given due consideration when we take measures to prevent detriment. Ibn Taymiyyah says: "When we consider a resulting detriment that may require the prohibition of something, we must also consider the need that may encourage making it permissible, desirable or even required.

---

9. Ibid, p. 41.

Whatever is outlawed to prevent detriment should be permitted when it ensures serving clear interests. Islam disapproves of one man and one woman being alone in an enclosed space or travelling together and disapproves of a man staring at a woman because all these may cause detriment. Islam prohibits a woman from travelling unless she is accompanied by her husband or a close relative. Yet all these prohibitions are put in place because of the detriment they cause. Should there be a preponderant interest dependent on such matters, they are deemed not to lead to detriment. It is a rule of Islamic law that when something leads to mixed results, consideration is given to what is more likely."

CHAPTER II

Women's Participation in Social Activity

Examples from the Prophet's Time

Every Muslim woman should conduct her life in the light of the guidance God has included in His revealed book as explained in practice by His Messenger. The practical examples we are now presenting to show women's participation in social activity are only cases reported for a particular purpose in the Qur'an or the Prophet's statements. If we were to compile all practical cases of women believers that occurred during the lifetimes of earlier prophets or Prophet Muhammad (peace be upon them all), we would have a collection of certain types of putting divine guidance into practice. There will always remain, however, wider room for its implementation in our own times and in the future. Divine guidance will always allow further and numerous ways of application, as suits different communities and generations.

In our discussion we will speak of two types of social activity. The first is undertaken by a group of individuals to bring about some results that are either good for themselves or for society in a religious or cultural area. The other type speaks of an activity voluntarily undertaken by an individual or a group of individuals to serve their community, either in the field of education, or to enjoin what is right and beneficial, or in what we nowadays call social work.

In modern society, women can play a major role in social activity. Therefore, we have made an effort to include statements relating to such social activity that occur in the Qur'an and in the two authentic anthologies of hadith by al-Bukhari and Muslim, including those already mentioned in the previous chapter and earlier volumes. We have also made sure to include texts that highlight women's social role, even though they might not involve mixing with men, in order to emphasise this role in all situations. Here are some examples that took place during the Prophet's lifetime.

1. Participation in Activities in the Mosque:

In worship:

Asmā' bint Abu Bakr reports: "The sun was eclipsed during the Prophet's lifetime... When I finished my business, I went over to the mosque where the Prophet was standing up in prayer. I joined the congregation, but he stayed up too long and I felt like sitting down. I looked and saw a woman who looked weak, and I thought that she was weaker than me. Therefore, I remained standing. He then bowed and stayed long in the bowing position. He then stood up and remained standing for a long while. Anyone who came in at that time would have thought that the Prophet had not bowed yet. The Prophet finished the prayer when the sun had fully reappeared. Addressing the congregation, he praised God as He deserves to be praised, then said..." (Related by al-Bukhari and Muslim, but Muslim's version is quoted here)

- IN EDUCATION:

  Fāṭimah bint Qays reports: "... I went to the mosque and joined the prayer with the Prophet... When he had finished his prayer, he sat on the platform smiling, and said: 'Let everyone stay in place. Do you know why I have asked you to come over?' They said that God and His Messenger knew best. He said: 'I have not asked you to come in order to give you an admonition of hope or fear. It is because Tamīm al-Dārī was a Christian, but he came over, pledged his allegiance and accepted Islam. He also told me something that is in full agreement of what I had told you about the Impostor..." (Related by Muslim)

- IN SOCIAL MEETINGS:

  Al-Rubayyiʿ bint Muʿawwidh ibn ʿAfrāʾ reports: "On 10 Muharram, the Prophet sent a message to the Anṣār's villages that whoever did not fast that day should complete the day fasting, and whoever began the day fasting should complete his fast. We used to fast on that day in the following years and we also encouraged our children to fast and made woollen dolls for them." (Related by al-Bukhari and Muslim) Muslim's version adds the following: "We would go to the mosque. If our young ones asked for food, we would give them a doll to distract them so that they could finish their fast."

We have limited ourselves here to one example for each of the three types of activity because in our discussion of mixing between men and women in the mosque, in Volume 2, we demonstrated that women used to go to the mosque for no less than 12 purposes. These included participation in different types of worship, such as congregational prayers, whether obligatory or voluntary, and taking part in educational functions such as listening to what the Prophet used to teach his companions. Women also attended public meetings in the mosque when these were called for and attended entertainment activities like the Abyssinians' folk dancing on Eid Day.

2. Participation in Public Functions:

☙ In receptions:

Abu Bakr reports: "... We arrived in Madinah at night. People argued over who would be God's Messenger's hosts. He said: 'I will stay at Bani al-Najjār, the maternal uncles of 'Abd al-Muṭṭalib, as a special gesture.' Men and women were on roof tops while children and servants were in the streets chanting: 'O Muhammad, God's Messenger! O Muhammad, God's Messenger.'" (Related by Muslim)

☙ In Eid Celebrations:

Umm 'Aṭiyyah reports: "We were ordered to go out to prayer on the day of Eid, including young, unmarried women. Even those who were menstruating went with us and stayed behind the congregation. They would glorify God as those praying glorified Him and they would take part in the supplication as did all the people. They, thus, hoped to share in the blessings of the day." (Related by al-Bukhari and Muslim)

☙ At weddings:

'Ā'ishah narrated: "... My mother, Umm Rūmān, came over... She took me inside where there were several women from the Anṣār. They said: 'With all goodness and blessings! With all future happiness.' She left me with them and they attended to my appearance. All of a sudden I saw God's Messenger and they gave me up to him..." (Related by al-Bukhari and Muslim)

In his commentary on this hadith Ibn Ḥajar mentions another version related by Ahmad, with a different chain of transmission. In this version 'Ā'ishah is quoted as saying: "My mother took me in. The Prophet was seated on his couch with a number of men and women present. She placed me on his lap and said: 'This is your wife, Messenger of God. May God bless her for you.' All men and women left, and my marriage was thus completed in our home."

Again we limited ourselves to one example of each type, as these and many others were given when we talked about men and women taking part in public function and celebrations. Every type of public function has its own distinctive characteristics. Receptions are purely social gatherings, while Eid celebrations combine a worship aspect, represented by people joining in God's glorification and in special prayer, with an educational one as people listen to the sermon, together with a social one as men, women and children join in such a blessed event. That celebration was like what we would call today a grand festival.

3. Participation in Educational Functions Outside the Mosque:

A SPECIAL SEMINAR FOR WOMEN:

Abu Sa'īd al-Khudrī narrated: "A woman came to the Prophet and said: 'Messenger of God, men have taken for themselves all that you teach. Could you please assign to us a day when we come to you and you teach us as God has taught you.' He told her that they could attend on a particular day in a particular place. When they did, he went to them and taught them whatever he did, before saying to them: 'Any one of you who suffers the death of three children, they will be like a shield keeping her away from hell.' One of them asked him: 'How about two children?' She repeated this twice. He said: 'Even two! Even two! Even two.'" (Related by al-Bukhari and Muslim)

☙ Teaching in the Prophet's wives' homes:

Sa'd ibn Hishām ibn 'Āmir asked Ibn 'Abbās how the Prophet offered his Witr Prayer. Ibn 'Abbās answered: "Let me tell you who knows that better than anyone on earth." He asked who that was. Ibn 'Abbās said: "It is 'Ā'ishah. Go to her and ask her then come back and tell me what she says." Sa'd continues his report: "I set out to go to her. I passed by Ḥakīm ibn Aflaḥ and asked him to come with me. He said: 'I shall never go to her because I advised her not to involve herself with either of these two groups[10] but she continues to do so.' I appealed to him by God to join me and he came with me. We sought permission to enter and she admitted us. When we were in, she asked: 'Is that Ḥakīm?'[11] He said: 'Yes.' She asked: 'Who is with you?' He said: 'Sa'd ibn Hishām.' She asked: 'Which Hishām?' He said: 'Hishām ibn 'Āmir.'[12] She prayed for mercy for him and spoke well of him. I said to her: Mother of the believers! Tell me about the Prophet's manners. She said: 'Do you not read the Qur'an?' I

10. The two groups were the supporters of 'Alī, the fourth Caliph, and the supporters of Ṭalḥah and al-Zubayr who demanded the punishment of 'Uthmān's assassins. The two groups were involved in what is known as the Battle of the Camel.
11. The Prophet's wives stayed behind a screen when they were visited by any men. People frequently went to them asking about the Prophet's guidance in a great variety of matters. They would speak to them, not knowing them. In this case, 'Ā'ishah recognized Ḥakīm by his voice.
12. Hishām was one of the Prophet's companions killed in the Battle of Uhud.

said I do. She said: 'The Prophet's manners were [a practical demonstration of] the Qur'an.' I thought I better leave and never ask anyone about anything until I die. Then I thought better and said: Tell me about the Prophet's night worship. She said..." (Related by Muslim)

4. Enjoining what is right:

God says in the Qur'an: "The believers, men and women, are friends to one another: They enjoin what is right and forbid what is wrong." (9: 71) Rashīd Riḍā says: "This verse makes it obligatory for men and women to enjoin what is right and forbid what is wrong... Women were aware of this and put it in practice." This is confirmed by the hadith related by al-Ṭabarānī which quotes Yaḥyā ibn Abi Sulaym as saying: "I saw Samrā' bint Nuhayk,[13] who was a companion of the Prophet, wearing thick garments and a thick head covering with a whip in her hand. She admonished people, enjoining what is right and forbidding whatever was wrong."

5. Voluntary Social Service:

☙ Giving assistance to the Muhājirīn:

Anas ibn Mālik reports: "The Muhājirīn from Makkah came to Madinah with no money. The Anṣār were the owners of the land there. They shared with them their annual harvests in return for their work... Umm Anas gave the Prophet the fruit of some date trees as a gift. He gave that over to Umm Ayman, Usāmah ibn Zayd's mother, the slave woman [who

13. Samrā' was appointed by 'Umar ibn al-Khaṭṭāb, the second Caliph, as the market supervisor in Makkah. This hadith refers to how she discharged her responsibilities, making sure that everything that took place in the market was in accordance with Islamic values.

looked after him when he was a young child]..." (Related by al-Bukhari and Muslim)

☙ Giving Hospitality:

Fāṭimah bint Qays reports: "... God's Messenger said to me: 'Move to Umm Sharīk's place' – Umm Sahrīk was a rich Anṣārī woman who donated much for God's cause and offered generous hospitality – I said I will do that. He, however, said: 'No, do not do that. Umm Sharīk entertains many guests...'" (Related by Muslim) In another version he described her as a woman who was visited by early migrants.

☙ Donating for the Mosque:

Jābir ibn 'Abdullāh reports that a woman from the Anṣār said to the Prophet: "Messenger of God! Shall I make you something to sit upon?"... She made him a platform. On the following Friday, he sat on it. (Related by al-Bukhari)

☙ Voluntary Service in the Mosque:

Abu Hurayrah reported that a black man or woman used to clean the mosque. [In his version al-Bukhari says, "In most probability, it was a woman."] Then that person died. The Prophet enquired and he was told of that person's death. He said: "Why have you not told me? Lead me to his [or her] grave." He went to the grave and prayed for her. (Related by al-Bukhari and Muslim) Commenting on this hadith, Ibn Ḥajar makes it clear that it is appropriate for a woman to volunteer for service in the mosque, as the Prophet approved of that woman's voluntary action.

☙ Voluntary Nursing:

Khārijah ibn Zayd reports that Umm al-'Alā', a woman from the Anṣār who had pledged allegiance to the Prophet, told him that when the Anṣār drew lots to host the Muhājirīn, they drew ʿUthmān ibn Maẓʿūn's name. "Soon afterwards ʿUthmān fell ill at our place. I nursed him until he died and we wrapped his body for burial…" (Related by al-Bukhari)

⁂ Nursing the Wounded:

Abu Ḥāzim reports that he was present when Sahl ibn Saʿd was asked about the wounds the Prophet received in battle. His answer was: "I certainly know who washed the Prophet's wound, who poured water on it and how he was treated. It was Fāṭimah, the Prophet's daughter who washed his wound while ʿAlī poured water, using his shield as a container. When Fāṭimah realized that the water only increased his bleeding, she took a small piece of a straw mat and burnt it, then she put it over the wound and stopped the bleeding. In that battle, one of the Prophet's front teeth was broken and he was wounded on his face. His head gear was also broken." (Related by al-Bukhari and Muslim)

Ibn Ḥajar adds that al-Ṭabarī relates on Abu Ḥāzim's authority that on the day of the Battle of Uhud when the unbelievers withdrew, Muslim women went out to help the Prophet's companions. Fāṭimah was among those who went out.

6. Women's Social Work with no Man Involved:

⁂ Voluntary Donations:

ʿĀ'ishah narrated that some of his wives asked the Prophet: "Who of us will be the first to die after you?" He said: "The one with the tallest hand." They took a stick to measure their hands and it was Sawdah who had the tallest hand. "However, we learnt [after Zaynab bint Jahsh's death], who was the first to die after him, that he was referring to charity. She was a woman who loved to be charitable." In another version, 'Ā'ishah describes Zaynab as "a woman who was most dedicated in what she did, donating its proceeds for God's sake." (Related by al-Bukhari and Muslim)

Jābir reports: "... The Prophet went to his wife Zaynab, and found her soaking a piece of leather to dye it..." (Related by Muslim)

Ibn Ḥajar adds: "... Al-Ḥākim relates in the chapter on the Prophet's Companion's Merits in his *al-Mustadrak* anthology, quoting 'Ā'ishah... 'Zaynab was skilled with handicraft. She used to dye and sew, and she donated much for God's sake.'" Al-Ḥākim says that this hadith meets Muslim's conditions of authenticity.

☙ Service for Neighbours:

Asmā' bint Abu Bakr reports: "Al-Zubayr married me when he had neither property nor servant on earth apart from a camel used to carry water and his horse. I used to feed the horse, draw the water, stitch the leather bucket and also make the dough. However, I was not good at making bread. Some of my neighbours of the Anṣār used to bake for me. They were good women..." (Related by al-Bukhari and Muslim)

☙ Lending Clothes for Special Occasions:

'Abd al-Wāḥid ibn Ayman reports: "I visited 'Ā'ishah and found her wearing a robe made of cotton, valued at five dirhams. She said: '... During the Prophet's lifetime, I had a robe of that kind. Whenever a woman from Madinah was being dressed for her wedding, she would send to me to borrow it." (Related by al-Bukhari)

ঙ Education:

Al-Shifā' bint 'Abdullāh reports: "The Prophet came in when I was with Ḥafṣah. He said to me: 'How about teaching this lady how to treat open sores like you taught her to write?'" (Related by Ahmad and Abu Dāwūd)

Women's Social Role in Contemporary Society

Contemporary societies are distinguished by certain aspects that have a considerable bearing on women's role and social activities. One most important aspect is the great advances made in education, its broad scopes and numerous disciplines, different stages and availability for boys and girls. All this has made women better able to take part in a wide range of social activities.

General education, together with the spread of the media and speedy transport, have contributed to the strengthening of community feeling and the formation of a variety of public institutions. In education, research institutes and specialised boards have been established; in the economic field, a variety of private and public sector companies have prospered; in different types of work, trade unions and professional associations; in politics, parties of different outlooks. It is only natural that a wide range of establishments should be formed to cover social work of every type. These are in need of the efforts of good women to be augmented by the efforts of good men.

On the other hand, some of our societies suffer from a general lack of progress and development, particularly in areas where poverty, ignorance, disease, wrongdoing and carelessness are widespread. To counter all this, there is a pressing need for increased social activity of all types. Such social activity is needed in all urban and rural areas. It should address the needs of both men and women so as to be effective in setting society on the road to progress.

In addition to all this, we note a new awareness of every individual's responsibility, man or woman, towards one's community as well as the awareness of the great importance of cooperation in discharging this responsibility.

Social Work in Modern Society

Every activity undertaken in an organised way and that aims to achieve some good for people in their social lives can be classified as Muslims' social work. This may fall in the area of enjoining whatever is right and prohibiting wrong, or it may be an educational, cultural or health activity, or indeed it may be in the fields of sports, leisure or enjoyment, or in providing help for the poor.

Every social activity, and indeed every human activity a Muslim does, including leisure and entertainment activities, comes under the overall umbrella of worship, in its broad sense of obedience to God and submission to His will. The only conditions that need to be met are that such activity should follow the line established by the Almighty and done with the right intention. God says in the Qur'an: "I have not created the jinn and mankind to any end other than they may worship Me." (51: 56)

One good and important advantage of social work is maintaining the dignity of the poor because such work offers them help in the form of services provided by public institutions, rather than a charity denoted by individuals, for whom the poor should be indebted.

Two types of people are directly involved in social work: those who contribute time, effort and money, in varying degrees, to ensure its efficiency, and the beneficiaries who are at the receiving end. A positive interaction between the two groups is most important. The ones in need must be helped so that they will learn, acquire skills, become productive and ultimately join those who contribute. A weak, unskilled or ignorant person can contribute nothing to his family or community. The aim should always be that those who are among the beneficiaries today will become contributors in the future.

One important objective of social work is to keep the gates of good work wide open so that every Muslim man and woman, whatever abilities and skills they may have, can make a contribution, whether material or in the form of advice and good counsel. From the first generation of Muslims, i.e. the Prophet's companions, we have such examples as Abu Masʿūd al-Anṣārī and Zaynab bint Jahsh. We mentioned how the latter used to work so that she could give her earnings in charity. When Abu Masʿūd heard the order to give to charity, he went to the market place and offered to carry people's goods. He was thus able to earn some money and make charitable donations.

Unlike other types of human activity, social work is open to both men and women. Indeed women's role in this field may be greater for a variety of reasons such as:

- Women are generally more compassionate and soft hearted.
- More women prefer to take up jobs as social workers, even though such preference may be based on the fact that such work is more suited to their own circumstances.
- Social work provides a wide field for housewives to take up responsibilities that ensure that they make a useful contribution to their community while using their spare time in a beneficial way that may also be enjoyable.
- Women are often better able to deliver the social services needed by other women, children or elderly people.

Social work offers the scope and ease for women to take part. In place, time and type of activities social work has clear advantages: a social institution is often active in the local community, and women can participate in it as suits their time and abilities.

ʿĀ'ishah gives us a fine description of a woman who provides a great role model in good work. It is useful to quote her description again: "... I have never seen a woman who is better in faith or more God-fearing or truthful in what she says or kind to relatives or charitable or more modest in her work through which she earns what she gives for charity, purely to please God, than Zaynab [bint Jahsh]." (Related by Muslim) Our women today cannot do much better than take Zaynab as a role model and come forward to offer their services to good social work. They will, thus, serve God's cause and earn His blessings.

Islamic Principles Relevant to Women's Social Work in Our Times

Principle One:

Muslim women are required to contribute to good work in their community just as men are required to do the same. God says in the Qur'an: "Believers! Bow down and prostrate yourselves, and worship your Lord alone, and do good so that you might be successful." (22: 77) It is most important that all necessary arrangements at the individual, family, community and government levels are put in place to enable women to play their role in society's progress. What is important is that the facilities to enable women to discharge their social and domestic responsibilities are provided. In most cases this is not difficult to achieve, as we suggested when we outlined the nature of social work. In the Qur'an we read God's words: "Anyone, be it man or woman, who does good deeds and is a believer, shall enter paradise and shall not suffer the least injustice." (4: 124) "The believers, men and women, are friends to one another: They enjoin what is right and forbid what is wrong." (9: 71) "Help one another in furthering righteousness and piety." (5: 2) "No good comes out of much of their secret talks; except for one who enjoins charity, or justice, or setting things right between people." (4: 114)

Al-Nuʿmān ibn Bashīr quotes the Prophet as saying: "In their mutual compassion, friendly feelings and sympathy, believers are like one body: if one organ suffers a complaint, the whole body shares in sleeplessness and fever." (Related by al-Bukhari and Muslim)

Abu Mūsā quotes the Prophet as saying: "In relations to one another, believers are like a building, each part strengthens the others... [The Prophet crossed his fingers to illustrate]." (Related by al-Bukhari and Muslim)

Jarīr ibn ʿAbdullāh reports: "... I went to the Prophet and said: 'I have come to give you my pledge as a Muslim.' He stipulated a condition that I should always give good counsel to every Muslim. I gave him my pledge on these terms." (Related by al-Bukhari and Muslim)

Tamīm al-Dārī narrated: "The Prophet said: 'Religion is sincerity.'[14] We asked to whom? He said: 'To God, His Book, His Messenger, the leaders of the Muslim community and to all Muslims.'" (Related by Muslim) Explaining this hadith, Ibn Ḥajar says: "*Naṣīḥah* to Muslims means being kind to them, doing what is of benefit to them, teaching them what brings them good, trying to prevent what is harmful, loving for them what one loves for oneself and steering them away from what one dislikes for oneself."

14. The Prophet used the Arabic term *naṣīḥah*, which carries several meanings. Its most common meaning is "good advice", which is clearly unsuitable in this context. It also means "probity, integrity, doing something good for a person, etc."

ʿAbdullāh ibn ʿUmar quotes the Prophet as saying: "A Muslim is a brother to every Muslim: he neither does an injustice to him nor lets him down. Whoever helps his brother in what he needs, God will help him get what he himself needs. Whoever eases the stress felt by a brother of his, God will reward him by easing the stress he feels on the Day of Judgement, and whoever shelters[15] a Muslim will receive shelter from God on the Day of Resurrection." (Related by al-Bukhari and Muslim) Ibn Ḥajar explains, "The term 'lets him down' means abandoning him when he is in a situation of difficulty or exposed to harm that may be caused by others. On the contrary, he should give him support and try to prevent such harm. This may be obligatory or recommended, according to the situation." We may add that it means 'to save him from any situation that may lead to harm or ruin'. Many types of good work come under this umbrella, such as saving a person from a killer disease, dire poverty, ignorance, or idleness.

Abu Mūsā quotes the Prophet as saying: "Every Muslim must give something to charity." His audience asked: "What if he has nothing to give?" He said: "He does some work with his hands and thus benefits himself and has something to give to charity." They asked: "What if he cannot or does not?" He said: "He can help someone in urgent need." They again said: "And what if he does not?" He said: "He can enjoin what is right and forbid what is wrong." Once more they said: "What if he does not do that?" He said: "He can at least refrain from evil. This will count as a charity." (Related by al-Bukhari and Muslim)

15. Here, the Prophet uses the verb *satara*, which means 'to give cover'. It conveys a broad sense of cover which includes "overlooking shortcomings, keeping someone's failings secret, particularly sins, etc. It also includes giving your poor brother material assistance so that his want is not exposed." It thus means giving shelter to avoid any type of exposure, provided that this helps the recipient in a good way.

Abu Hurayrah quotes the Prophet as saying: "Every joint in a person's body has an obligation to do a charity with every sunrise: To ensure fairness between two people, or help a person get on top of his mount, or help him in putting his luggage on the back of his animal – every such thing counts as a charity. A kindly word is a charity. Every step on the way to prayers is a charity, and removing harmful objects from people's way is an act of charity." (Related by al-Bukhari and Muslim)

Abu Dharr narrated: "I asked the Prophet (peace be upon him) which actions are best. He said: 'To believe in God and to strive for His cause.' I said: 'What slaves are best to set free?' He answered: 'The highest in price and the best valued by their owners.' I asked: 'What if I cannot do that?' He said: 'To help someone who is at a loss or to do something for someone who is incapable.' I further asked: 'And if I do not do that?' He said: 'To spare people from evil. This is an act of charity which you do to yourself.'" (Related by al-Bukhari and Muslim)

'Abdullāh ibn 'Amr narrated that God's Messenger said: "There are forty different acts of charity, the best of which is to give a goat away.[16] Anyone who maintains any of these acts purely for God's reward and in full confidence of its promise will be certain to be admitted by God into heaven." (Related by al-Bukhari)

Anas quotes the Prophet as saying: "Whenever a Muslim plants a tree or some other plant, and a bird or a human being or an animal eats of it, it will count as an act of charity for him." (Related by al-Bukhari and Muslim)

16. The special phrase the Prophet uses in this hadith means to give a goat to a poor person so that he benefits by its milk for a while and then returns the goat to its owner.

Abu Hurayrah narrated that "God's Messenger (peace be upon him) said: 'Faith has seventy-odd aspects, the highest of which is to declare that there is no deity other than God and the lowest is to remove harm from people's way. Modesty is an aspect of faith.'" (Related by Muslim)

Abu Hurayrah narrated that the Prophet said: "A man was walking along his way when he found a thorny branch of a tree. He picked it up. God was thankful for his action and He forgave him his sins."[17] (Related by al-Bukhari and Muslim)

Abu Hurayrah quotes the following story as he heard it from the Prophet: "'As a man was walking along, he felt extremely thirsty. He found a well and he went down into it and drank. As he came up, he saw a dog panting hard, almost eating the dust because of his thirst. He thought: 'This dog is as thirsty as I have just been.' He went down the well again, filled his shoe with water holding it by his mouth, went up again and put it before the dog to drink. God thanked him for his action by forgiving him his sins.' The Prophet's companions asked: 'Messenger of God! Will we be rewarded for a kindness to animals?' He said: 'Whatever kindness you do to a living creature will earn you a reward.'" (Related by al-Bukhari and Muslim)

Abu Hurayrah quotes the Prophet as saying: "As a dog was walking round a well, almost dying of thirst, a prostitute from among the Children of Israel saw him. She took off her shoe and used it to give

---

17. As we all tend to make mistakes and even the most pious among us commit the odd offence, and as we all fall short of thanking God enough for His favours, we are always in need of God's forgiveness. The Prophet describes here a simple act that earned a person forgiveness for his past sins. This was no more than picking up a thorny branch so that it would not hurt any passer by. This is an act of kindness done to others whom the person concerned does not know. Thereby, it is for the community as a whole.

him water to drink. She was forgiven in reward for her kindness."[18] (Related by al-Bukhari and Muslim)

'Adiy ibn Ḥātim quotes the Prophet as saying: "Every single one of you shall be spoken to by his Lord, with no interpreter between them. He will look to his right and find nothing except his actions, and he will look to his left but he sees nothing other than his actions. He will then look in front of him but he sees nothing except hell fire facing him. Spare yourselves the torment of fire, even by half a date."[19] (Related by al-Bukhari and Muslim) Another version of this hadith adds: "If you cannot find that, then by a word of kindness."

It should be noted that although most of these texts are expressed in the masculine form, they all include both men and women.

Principle Two:

> Good action, as also cooperation in doing what is good, is recommended in all situations. However, it may become a personal duty in some cases or a collective duty in others. Every thoughtful Muslim woman should do her best in identifying the areas of collective duties for women, particularly in the social field, such as providing care for other women and children, particularly orphans.

The area of good action and kindness to people, which is recommended in all situations, is very wide. It is open to the discretion of good people in every community who can assess needs and how they can help to meet them. We have already given many examples and their

18. This hadith shows that even a small kindness, given in pure sincerity and with no expectation of any return, can outweigh a cardinal sin.
19. This hadith illustrates the great value Islam attaches to charity and kindness. A very small act of charity can save a person from hell, provided that it is done with sincerity and dedication.

relevant texts under Principle One. We also gave other examples when we cited cases of women's participation in social work during the Prophet's lifetime.

It is definitely recommended for women to take part in social work that aims to fulfil noble objectives, putting into it both time and effort. Likewise, women with money are recommended to donate to such work. A woman who has no money of her own may contribute from her husband's money in a reasonable way or within the limits of what is known to be acceptable.

Asmā' reports: "I said to the Prophet that I had nothing other than what al-Zubayr [her husband] had given me. Should I give to charity out of that? He said: 'Yes, give to charity. Do not hold on to what you have without giving to others, for then good things will be withheld from you.'" (Related by al-Bukhari and Muslim) Another version of this hadith mentions that the Prophet said to her: "Give to charity in a reasonable way, as long as you can afford that."

'Ā'ishah narrated that the Prophet said: "When a woman gives away some of the food of her family, in a reasonable way, she earns a reward for what she has given and her husband is also given a reward for having earned it." (Related by al-Bukhari and Muslim)

Collective social duties are often lost sight of in backward communities where necessities and needs that are essential for all people are numerous, while the charitable spirit that motivates people to give is weakened. As they try to map their way to progress, our communities desperately need to nurture in every individual, man and woman, the sense of responsibility towards helping their community meet its needs, let alone its vital necessities. We need to fully understand that unless these needs are met, then we all, men and women, are party to the crime of lingering backwardness our communities endure, sitting back when the whole community needs to strive hard in order to achieve progress. This means that we are not doing our duty, not doing jihad for God's cause, namely the progress of our community. On the Day of Judgement, all of us, men and women, will be accountable to God for this negligence of our duty. It may happen that people evade their collective duties due to the ignorance that results from the sort of isolation in which many women live. People may be ignorant of the nature of needs and essential requirements, as well as the dire consequences of not meeting them, and they may also be totally unaware of the ways and means of addressing such needs and meeting requirements. The ultimate result is that people thus fall short of discharging their responsibilities. What we must realize is that collective duties may become the personal duties of those who are aware of them and their importance, and who are able to fulfil them. If some of these collective duties are required of men in the first place, yet in a case of general backwardness and lack of enough male ability and understanding, these duties become applicable to women who are endowed with such understanding and ability. It may be useful here to refer to the views of Imam al-Ḥaramayn al-Juwaynī on the serious consequences of neglecting collective duties which we quoted under Principle Eight relevant to women's professional work.

Principle Three:

> Every Muslim woman is recommended to take part in social work when such participation brings good returns to her or helps her to improve herself intellectually, spiritually or socially.

In reference to the Prophet's wives, God says in the Qur'an: "Bear in mind all that is recited in your homes of God's revelations and wisdom; for God is unfathomable in His wisdom, all aware." (33: 34) 'Ā'ishah narrated: "When the final ten nights of Ramadan began, the Prophet would refrain from having sex with his wives, spend most of the night in worship and would awake his family [for night worship]." (Related by al-Bukhari and Muslim)

The Qur'anic verse above refers to what a woman should do in order to improve herself, reciting the Qur'an, learning its meanings and grasping the wisdom it contains. The hadith encourages women to take part in night worship, particularly during the last third of the month of Ramadan. In Volume 2, we discussed at length women's participation in mosque activities during the Prophet's lifetime. They were keen to take part in worship and educational activities, staying for some days in the mosque where their time is devoted to voluntary worship, attending *Tarāwīḥ* Prayers and the prayer during a solar eclipse, in addition to her regular attendance of Friday Prayer.

Friday Prayer provides a weekly dose of spiritual, intellectual and social nourishment for all believers who attend it. Hence, it is particularly important for women to be present. Yet negligence of this prayer, for a variety of reasons, is widespread among women. In modern parlance, this prayer represents a regular social activity that can play an important role in bringing women out of their social isolation and help in increasing their awareness and maturity. This is particularly true when the sermon before the prayer tackles social, economic or political issues affecting the local community or the Muslim world at large, in addition to religious preaching.

We, therefore, need to discuss the views of some scholars of old who preferred that women should stay at home and not attend Friday Prayer, as also cite a number of hadiths and views recommending that women should rather attend this prayer. We will also add some notions that we believe to be universally accepted in this context.

1. In his book *al-Majmū'*, Imam al-Nawawī says: "Scholars of our school of thought mention that those who are exempt from attending Friday Prayer are of two types: the first includes those whose reasons

for exemption are expected to be removed, such as slaves, travellers or sick people. These people can pray Ẓuhr[20] before Friday Prayer is offered in the mosque, but it is better that they should delay praying it until they have given up on their ability to attend Friday Prayer... The other type are the ones whose reasons will not be removed, such as women and those whose illnesses are chronic and incurable. Two views are given in respect of this second type. The weightier view is that they are recommended to pray Ẓuhr at the beginning of its time, to gain the advantage of praying early. The other view is that it is better that they should delay praying Ẓuhr until the Friday Prayer is over, just as the first type. This is because they are physically able to attend the Friday Prayer, which is the one required of those who are fully fit. Hence, it should be the one offered first. These scholars add that even a person who is exempt from Friday Prayer is recommended to attend it if he can, even though he might have prayed Ẓuhr, because it is the more important prayer... As we said, Ẓuhr Prayer remains obligatory for those who are exempt from offering Friday Prayer. If they pray Ẓuhr, they discharge their duty. If they do not but offer Friday Prayer instead, that is acceptable and it is enough to discharge their duty, according to all scholars... It may be asked why those people whose obligation it is to pray Ẓuhr are required to offer four *rak'ahs* [which is the normal Ẓuhr Prayer] but then offer Friday Prayer consisting of two *rak'ahs* only? The answer is that Friday Prayer is the higher prayer, despite its being shorter. Hence it is required of all those who have no special circumstances to exempt them. Only those who have excuses requiring reduction in duty are given such exemption. If any of these takes the trouble to offer it, he does well and his action is accepted. It is like the person who is ill standing up in prayer despite being allowed to pray seated,

20. Ẓuhr Prayer is the one offered after midday on all days of the week except Friday, when it is replaced by Friday Prayer, which is different in length and preceded by a sermon. Hence the discussion here speaks of the two as mutually exclusive.

or one who performs the ablutions and washes his feet instead of wiping over his socks."

Such are the rulings applicable to those who are exempt from attending Friday Prayers. Al-Shirāzī, in *al-Muhadhdhab*, and al-Nawawī, in *al-Majmū'*, make an exception in the case of young and mature women who are attractive. Both say that it is recommended such women do not attend the Friday Prayers as also all prayers in the mosque. The evidence cited by al-Shirāzī relies on a report that attributes to the Prophet a statement saying that he ordered women not to attend the mosque 'apart from an elderly woman advanced in years'. Al-Nawawī comments that this hadith is 'strange', related by al-Bayhaqī with a chain of transmission that is poor in authenticity and attributed to 'Abdullāh ibn Mas'ūd without quoting the Prophet. The hadith in full says: "No woman offers a prayer better than praying at home, except for the two mosques in Makkah and Madinah, apart from an elderly woman advanced in years."

The fact that this hadith is poor in authenticity is enough to dismiss it as a basis for evidence. Moreover, when we examine its text we realize that it does not include any prohibition of women's attendance of congregational prayers in mosques. It simply says that praying at home is better for women. Al-Nawawī also cites 'Ā'ishah's statement: "Had the Prophet seen what women have perpetrated, he would have stopped them like the Israelite women were stopped." (Related by al-Bukhari and Muslim) In Muslim's version the statement reads, "He would have stopped them from attending the mosque." The best comment on this statement is that given by the eminent Ḥanbalī scholar, Ibn Qudāmah, who says: "It is the Prophet's tradition that is better followed. 'Ā'ishah's statement applies only to those who have perpetrated what is unacceptable from the Islamic point of view. Such women are better advised not to go out."

We would like to add that what 'Ā'ishah said should be taken as a reprimand to those women who perpetrated what is unacceptable.

It cannot abrogate the Prophet's order: "Do not deny women their share of the mosques." Can any statement by anyone, regardless of their being of the highest calibre in their conduct and knowledge, be construed as having the ability or knowledge to abrogate the Prophet's tradition?

We see how the evidence cited by scholars who prefer women not to attend Friday Prayer does not stand up to proper examination. Therefore, the rulings applicable to those who are exempt from this prayer also apply to women. These are that those exempt are still recommended to attend Friday Prayer when they can. Although it consists of two *rak'ah*s only, it is still preferable to Ẓuhr Prayer. Hence, it is obligatory for those who have no reason to exempt themselves. In other words, an exempted person does well to dispense with his exemption so as to attend it. In confirming this view, al-Sarakhsī, a leading Ḥanafī scholar, says: "People travelling, slaves, women and the sick who attend Friday Prayer do well, as evidenced by the hadith reported by al-Ḥasan: 'Women used to attend Friday Prayer during the Prophet's lifetime. They were told not to wear perfume when they went to the mosque.' Their exemption is not due to any factor relating to the prayer itself, but rather to remove any inconvenience. Should they put up with such inconvenience and attend, they are like all those who offer the Friday Prayer."

2. It is reported by 'Abdullāh ibn 'Umar that the Prophet said: "Any man or woman who attends the Friday Prayer should have a bath beforehand." (Related by Ibn Khuzaymah) This hadith provides a clear indication that women are welcome to attend Friday Prayers. 'Amrah bint 'Abd al-Raḥmān's sister reports: "I learnt the surah starting '*Qāf*. By the glorious Qur'an'[21] from the Prophet's mouth on Fridays as he used to recite it on the platform every Friday." (Related

21. This is Surah 50 of the Qur'an. The Prophet used to recite it frequently on Fridays as his sermons.

by Muslim) This hadith clearly states that women used to regularly attend Friday Prayers during the Prophet's lifetime. Another hadith states: "Friday Prayer is a duty incumbent on every Muslim in a community, except for four types who are exempt: a slave, a woman, a child, and a sick person." This hadith implies that attending Friday Prayers is not obligatory for women. Imam Mālik is quoted to have said: "Anyone, other than men, who wants to attend the Friday Prayer to benefit by it should have a bath before and observe all the good manners that are recommended for such attendance." Mālik's statement implies that there is a benefit to be sought by women through attending Friday Prayers.

3. Bearing in mind that attending the Friday Prayers is permissible, though not obligatory, for women, and that women used to attend it during the Prophet's lifetime, and that there is benefit they gain by such attendance through listening to the sermon and recitation of the Qur'an, as well as meeting other women and cooperating with them in good action, we can advisedly say that such attendance is clearly recommended for women. This recommendation is further strengthened by several considerations, including:

- No woman is less in need than any man of listening to a sermon every Friday. The sermon may tackle a social problem that cannot be solved without community cooperation or it may address a political issue that the community needs to be made aware of.
- Although women are no less in need of admonition than men, they may be unable to attend the Friday Prayer for one week or several weeks because they happen to be menstruating or suffering postnatal discharge, or have young children who need to be looked after and cannot be left alone at home, thus, women may miss out on much benefit because of their special circumstances.

- The Prophet issued an emphatic order to all women, including the young and adolescent, to attend the Eid Prayer. Friday Prayer shares certain aspects of Eid Prayer, as both include a sermon and are attended by a large gathering. Moreover, it is an occasion that imparts a status of honour to Friday, which is a special day in Islam. All this puts this prayer in a middle position between the normal five obligatory prayers and the Eid Prayer.

All this makes clear that God has not made it obligatory for women to attend Friday Prayers so as not to place a heavy burden on them. There is no doubt, however, that every woman should be keen to attend this prayer, and that she should be helped in this by her husband or guardian. It is a beneficial practice which should be promoted by all.

Principle Four:

> It is perfectly permissible for women to be involved in social and leisure activities so as to enjoy herself within what is good and permissible. Taking part in such activities is even encouraged if it helps women to discharge their responsibilities.

We have already cited a number of cases that took place during the Prophet's lifetime clearly indicating that women took part in leisure activities that took place both inside or outside the mosque.

Principle Five:

> It is important to include among the objectives of general education of Muslim boys and girls that they should be able to take part in some type of beneficial social work. Moreover, young people, boys and girls alike, should understand that

> their responsibilities, for which they are accountable before God, are not limited to their families but include the whole community whenever they have something to offer.

To achieve this objective, education curricula must include three elements: 1) consolidation of the moral motive which is outlined by several texts included under Principle One; 2) a thorough study of the local community and its needs; and 3) practical training in community service within the school and through school activity in the first place, and also in society through the local social institutions.

Principle Six:

> Every woman should make full use of her time, endeavouring to be of benefit to her community. She should not be idle at any stage of her life. Therefore, she should always use her spare time in some beneficial activity. Needless to say, social work provides wide scope for a variety of beneficial activities.

Al-Muhallab says: "... A woman may volunteer to do what she likes of recommended actions, other than what is incumbent on her, without need for her husband's permission, if her action neither causes him harm nor stops him from fulfilling his duties. It is not open to any husband to stop his wife doing something for God's sake if she has started it without his permission."

Principle Seven:

> It is recommended for a Muslim man to help his wife in her domestic duties when she is heavily involved in recommended social work. Should such social work be obligatory, then providing such help becomes his duty.

We have cited enough evidence in support of this under Principle Eight of women's professional work. A man shares with his wife the reward of her social work when he encourages her to do it. His reward is increased in relation to the help and encouragement he gives her.

We have also quoted the hadith that says: "When a woman gives away some of the food of her family, in a reasonable way, she earns a reward for what she has given and her husband is also given a reward for having earned it." (Related by al-Bukhari and Muslim) On the basis of this hadith we may add that although a married woman's time is due to her family in the first place, when she takes part in beneficial social work, putting into it some of her time, in a reasonable way, she earns a reward for what she does. What is more is that her husband also earns a reward for taking care of his family home and earning their living on the one hand, and for tolerating his wife's absence on the other.

Principle Eight:

> The Muslim community bears a collective responsibility to provide the ways and means that enable women to discharge their duties towards their community, in addition to their family duties.

God says in the Qur'an: "The believers, men and women, are friends to one another." (9: 71) Al-Nuʿmān ibn Bashīr quotes the Prophet as saying: "In their mutual compassion, friendly feelings and sympathy, believers are like one body: if one organ suffers a complaint, the whole body shares in sleeplessness and fever." (Related by al-Bukhari and Muslim)

At both the individual and institutional levels, a Muslim community is characterised by mutual sympathy and compassion. In every Muslim community, good people should join efforts in a positive initiative that aims to achieve the following:

- Establishing in every locality social institutions that provide a wide scope for women's participation in serving the community, in whatever way and measure they can. These institutions may be composed of women only or may be ones in which both men and women participate;
- Encouraging women to play a role in serving the community, putting before them an outline of such a role and their responsibilities. The media and educational institutes should play a vital role in spreading such awareness;
- Encouraging all women to attend various social activities organised by social institutions, including educational, health and cooperative activities;
- Calling on men to help women participate in social activities, whether by contributing to it or benefiting by it.

Principle Nine:

> Every Muslim government is responsible for providing suitable instruction and encouragement to women to participate in productive and beneficial social work.

ʿAbdullāh ibn ʿUmar quotes the Prophet as saying: "Every one of you is a shepherd and accountable for those under his care. The ruler is a shepherd and he is responsible for his subjects." (Related by al-Bukhari and Muslim) This responsibility can be fulfilled in a variety of ways, including:

- Using the media, which is normally under government supervision, to encourage women to contribute to the progress of society, either through the formation of social institutions that are exclusive to women, or through participation in existing institutions.
- Facilitating the formation of social institutions that undertake different cultural, social and sports activities, either for women

only or ones in which women can play active roles. This should be augmented by providing every possible assistance to such institutions to enable them to function effectively.

- Encouraging women who work in government departments to play a role in social work, either by reducing their working hours or by giving them social leave on the same lines as study leaves, when they are heavily involved in such work.

Principle Ten:

> When women's participation in social activities involves bringing them and men together, both men and women must observe the Islamic values applicable in such situations, which we outlined earlier in this book. By way of reminder we cite here the needs to dress modestly, lower one's gaze, avoiding situations where one man is alone with one woman in an enclosed area as well as congestion and situations that lead to suspicion.

Questions may, however, arise here. If some of these values are not observed in existing social institutions, should we forego the beneficial objectives served by such institutions and ask Muslim women to refrain from taking part in them? Or, should we continue to promote such objectives while we work hard to ensure that Islamic values are observed? The fundamental Islamic principles require us to balance needs and benefits against resulting harm and to weigh pros and cons in every situation. We need to remind ourselves of what Ibn Taymiyyah says in this regard, which was quoted at the end of Chapter One:

- When we consider a resulting detriment that may require the prohibition of something, we must also consider the need that may encourage making it permissible, desirable or even required.

- Whatever is outlawed to prevent detriment should be permitted when it ensures serving clear interests. Islam disapproves of one man and one woman being alone in an enclosed space, or travelling together, and disapproves of a man staring at a woman, because all these may cause detriment. Islam prohibits a woman from travelling unless she is accompanied by her husband or a close relative. Yet all these prohibitions are put in place because of the detriment they cause. Should there be a preponderant interest dependent on such matters, they are deemed not to lead to detriment.
- It is a rule of Islamic law that when something leads to mixed results, consideration is given to what is more likely.

CHAPTER III

Political Participation by Muslim Women

Examples from the Prophet's Time

Islam aims to bring about a fundamental change in beliefs, morality, social conditions and government. Hence, in their attitude to the world of ignorance surrounding them, the early Muslims in Makkah were akin to the most revolutionary type of political parties that stand in opposition to government in a modern state. Generally speaking, religious activity is seen to fall within the wider area of social activity. However, this is true only when religious activity is limited to personal interaction between individual members of society. Should religious activity itself address political authority, standing in opposition to it, let alone advocating a revolution against it, then it becomes in modern parlance, a political activity. Such activity can be construed to include political activity wherein the then new faith of Islam was adopted. People sought to know about it so as to make up their minds concerning it, joined the Muslim community, took an interest in the fortunes of the new faith and advocated it, suffering persecution for adopting it, migrated for its sake and joined the struggle to defend and establish it in society.

Women can play a very important role in political activity in modern society. Therefore, we present texts from the Qur'an and the two authentic hadith anthologies of al-Bukhari and Muslim that touch on such activity, even though they may not involve mixing with men. Our aim is to highlight the importance of women's political participation.

One: In the Land of Disbelief

'Ā'ishah narrated:

> The first aspect of revelation to God's Messenger was that his dreams came true. Whatever vision he might have had in his sleep would occur as he had seen... The angel came to him and said: "Read, in the name of Your Lord Who created – created man out of a clinging cell mass. Read – for your Lord is the most Bountiful One, Who has taught the use of the pen, taught man what he did not know." The Prophet returned home to Khadījah, trembling, and said: "Wrap me! Wrap me!" They wrapped him and his fear subsided. He turned to Khadījah and exclaimed: "What has happened to me?" He related to her what happened and said: "I fear for myself," and Khadījah replied: "You have nothing to fear; be calm and relax. God will not let you suffer humiliation, because you are kind to your relatives, you speak the truth, you assist anyone in need, you are hospitable to your guest and you help in every just cause." Then she took him to Waraqah ibn Nawfal, her paternal cousin who was a Christian convert and a scholar with a good knowledge of Arabic, Hebrew and the Bible. He had lost his eyesight, as he had grown very old.

> Khadījah said to Waraqah: "Cousin, would you like to hear what your nephew has to say?" [Waraqah was not, in fact, the Prophet's uncle. Khadījah's reference to Muhammad as his nephew was in accordance with the standards of politeness which prevailed in Arabia at the time.] Waraqah said: "Well, nephew, what have you seen?" The Prophet related to him what he saw. When he had finished, Waraqah said: "It is the same revelation as was sent down to Moses. I wish I was a young man so that I might be alive when your people turn you away from this city." The Prophet exclaimed: "Would they turn me away?" Waraqah answered: "Yes! No man has ever preached a message like yours and was not met with enmity. If I live till that day, I will certainly give you all my support." But Waraqah died soon thereafter. (Related by al-Bukhari and Muslim)

We see how Khadījah strengthens the Prophet, saying words that combine maturity, love, compassion, profound respect with a logical analysis that confirms the truth of what he had experienced. She then takes steps to investigate the situation, referring to a good authority who confirms the truth of the new faith. She then becomes the first person to embrace it, believing in God's oneness. Hers was a rational attitude endowed with wisdom.

This reminds us of the attitude of another woman who was among the very early Muslims, when Islam was still in its early days of secrecy. She was very cautious when dealing with her people who were opposed to the new faith, but she was also intelligent and resourceful in providing help to her fledgling and oppressed community. Abu Bakr addressed the people of Quraysh sitting around the Ka'bah, surrounded by the Muslims who then numbered 38 people. The unbelievers beat him hard until he fell down and was then carried home, unconscious and so unable to walk. When he woke up, he asked: "What happened to God's Messenger?" His mother said:

"I have no knowledge of what happened to your friend." He said to her: "Go to Umm Jamīl bint al-Khaṭṭāb and ask her about him." She went to her and said: "Abu Bakr sent me to enquire of you about Muhammad ibn 'Abdullāh." Umm Jamīl said: "I know neither Abu Bakr nor Muhammad ibn 'Abdullāh. However, I am willing to come with you, if you wish." The two women went together to Abu Bakr. When Umm Jamīl saw him in his condition, almost close to death, she said: "Those who have done this to you are indeed wicked unbelievers. I hope that God will punish them for what they have done to you." He asked her what happened to the Prophet. She said: "Here is your mother listening to our conversation." He said: "Do not worry about her." She said: "He is fine and safe." He asked where he was and she replied that he was in al-Arqam's home. He said: "I pledge to God that I shall not eat or drink anything unless I go and see him." They told him to wait until the evening. Then when it was all quiet, they took him out, both supporting him as he walked up to the place where the Prophet was staying. The Prophet bent and kissed him, and the Muslims with him welcomed him warmly, making him comfortable.

Quick to Embrace the New Faith

AHEAD OF HER FATHER:

'Ā'ishah said that both Umm Ḥabībah bint Abu Sufyān and Umm Salamah spoke about a church they saw in Abyssinia. (Related by al-Bukhari) This hadith clearly indicates that Umm Ḥabībah was one of the Muslims who migrated to Abyssinia in Year 5 of the start of the Islamic message. Her father continued to resist Islam until shortly before Makkah fell to Islam, 21 years into its history. It is useful to relate the following story of how she dealt with her father before he accepted Islam. We should remember that Umm Ḥabībah was married to the Prophet after her first husband died whilst they were in Abyssinia.

Abu Sufyān came to Madinah, fearing that the Prophet would invade Makkah after the Quraysh had flagrantly violated the peace agreement between them and the Muslims. His mission was to try to dissuade the Prophet from taking any retaliatory action by offering to increase the duration of the peace agreement. When he spoke to the Prophet on this, the Prophet did not enter into any discussion with him. Abu Sufyān then went to his daughter, Umm Ḥabībah. He entered her room and, behaving like any father in his daughter's house, proceeded to sit down on the Prophet's mattress. Umm Ḥabībah was faster than him – she folded the mattress and took it away. Surprised, Abu Sufyān asked: "I am not quite sure, child, whether you think that I am above sitting on your mattress or that it is too good for me." She put it to him quite frankly: "It is the mattress of God's Messenger and since you are an idolater you are impure. Hence, I do not want you to sit on the mattress of God's Messenger, (peace be upon him)." That was a totally unexpected blow for Abu Sufyān. He could not have imagined that his own daughter would humiliate him in this way. He said: "I am certain some harm has befallen you since you left me, daughter."

Ahead of her brother:

Sa'īd ibn Zayd reports: "I was in a situation when 'Umar had tied me up because I embraced Islam, when he had not yet done so." (Related by al-Bukhari) Another version mentions that both Sa'īd and his wife, 'Umar's sister, were tied up. Ibn Ḥajar explains that "'Umar accepted Islam sometime after his sister, Fāṭimah, and her husband had done so. In fact, the first thought of embracing Islam only occurred to 'Umar after he had listened to the Qur'an being recited in her house."

Ahead of her husband:

Ibn 'Abbās reports: "Both my mother and I were among the weaker elements: I as a child and my mother as a woman." (Related by al-Bukhari) Ibn Ḥajar comments: "His mother was Lubābah bint al-Ḥārith, better known as Umm al-Faḍl, as al-Faḍl was her eldest son." Al-Bukhari mentions that 'Abdullāh ibn 'Abbās did not follow his father in keeping with his people's old religion. This is based on the assumption that al-'Abbās embraced Islam after the Battle of Badr, but scholars differ on this point. What is certain is that he migrated shortly before Makkah fell to Islam and he joined the Prophet as he moved to take it over.

Ibn 'Abbās's statement refers to the Qur'anic verse that states: "And why should you not fight in the cause of God and the utterly helpless men, women and children who are crying, 'Our Lord! Deliver us from this land whose people are oppressors, and send forth to us, out of Your grace, a protector, and send us one that will help us.'" (4: 75)

Al-Miswar ibn Makhramah reports: "...The Prophet mentioned that he had a son-in-law from the clan of 'Abd Shams (whose name was Abu al-'Āṣ ibn al-Rabī') and he praised him for being a good son-in-law. He also said: 'He spoke to me and he was truthful, and when he gave me a promise he was true to his word.'" (Related by al-Bukhari and Muslim) Ibn Ḥajar comments: "Abu al-'Āṣ ibn al-Rabī' married Zaynab, the Prophet's eldest daughter, before the start of revelations. She accepted Islam but he did not. He fell prisoner to the Muslims during the Battle of Badr. Zaynab sent the ransom to free him. The Prophet also made it a condition of his release that he would send Zaynab to him. He fulfilled his promise sending his wife to the Prophet. It is to this promise that the Prophet refers in this hadith.

Another woman that preceded her husband in accepting Islam was Ḥawwā' bint Yazīd of the Anṣār. She embraced Islam at an early date, when the Prophet was still in Makkah. Her husband used to treat her very badly. The Prophet went to see him and said to him: "Abu

Yazīd! I have learnt that you have been ill-treating your wife, Ḥawwā' ever since she chose a religion different to yours. Fear God and do me a kindness by refraining from treating her badly." He said: "I will indeed. I will only do what you like and will treat her well."

Likewise, Umm Sulaym accepted Islam before her first husband, Mālik ibn al-Naḍr, Anas's father. At the time, her husband was away. When he returned, he asked her: "Have you renounced your religion?" She said: "I did not renounce anything. I only believed in this Prophet." She started to teach her son, Anas, to say that there is no deity other than God and that Muhammad is God's Messenger. His father said to her: "Do not force my son away from my line." She said: "I am not forcing him to do anything." Mālik then went out and someone who was hostile towards him killed him.

A woman may choose to believe together with her husband, but when such a step is taken by free choice, she may be firm in her faith despite any change of heart her husband might have. For example, Umm Ḥabībah was married to 'Ubaydillāh ibn Jaḥsh, and they both migrated to Abyssinia. He, however, renounced Islam and became a Christian before dying there. Umm Ḥabībah remained a Muslim throughout, later marrying the Prophet.

Ahead of her masters

'Ammār ibn Yāsir reports: "I saw the Prophet when he had none other than five slaves, two women and Abu Bakr." This means that despite a slave woman's very weak position in society, she went ahead, despite her masters' opposition, and embraced the new faith. She would, thus, rise to a new height. Among such slave women were Ḥamāmah, Umm 'Ubays, Zinnīrah, al-Nahdiyyah and her daughter, and a slave woman belonging to the 'Adiy clan. We will mention these again shortly.

Marwān and al-Miswar ibn Makhramah report: "Umm Kulthūm bint 'Uqbah ibn Abi Mu'ayṭ was among those who went over to join the Prophet during this period (after the signing of the al-Hudaybiyah peace agreement). She was a young woman who had recently attained puberty. Her people came over to Madinah requesting the Prophet to return her, but he refused their request." (Related by al-Bukhari) Ibn Sa'd reported in *al-Ṭabaqāt al-Kubrā*: "We do not know of any woman from the Quraysh who had left her family, migrating to join the Prophet other than Umm Kulthūm bint 'Uqbah. Her two brothers, al-Walīd and 'Imārah, followed her to Madinah trying to have her returned.

Believers Facing Persecution

Sa'īd ibn Zayd reports: "I was in a situation when 'Umar had tied me up because I embraced Islam, when he had not yet done so." (Related by al-Bukhari) Al-Bukhari relates this hadith under several headings, one of which is, 'Those preferring to be beaten, killed or humiliated rather than to disbelieve'. Ibn Ḥajar comments that the hadith is obviously relevant here because Sa'īd and his wife, Fāṭimah, chose humiliation over disbelief. What 'Umar did to Sa'īd was to publicise his humiliation by tying him up, seeking to force him to renounce his faith. Sa'īd was married to 'Umar's sister and Sa'īd's father was 'Umar's own cousin. 'Umar, however, later accepted Islam.

A short while ago, we quoted a hadith reported by 'Ammār who says: "I saw the Prophet when he had none other than five slaves, two women and Abu Bakr." 'Ammār's mother, Sumayyah, was one of those five slaves. Ibn Ḥajar says: "It must be that among those five slaves were 'Ammār and his parents. All three were tortured for having accepted Islam. His mother was the first martyr in Islamic history when Abu Jahl killed her with his spear."

Biographies of the Prophet mention that when Abu Bakr passed by a slave being tortured, he would buy that slave and set him or her free. Among those he freed were Bilāl and his mother Ḥamāmah, as he did with Umm ʿUbays, Zinnīrah, al-Nahdiyyah and her daughter, and a slave woman belonging to the ʿAdiy clan whom ʿUmar used to torture before he accepted Islam.

Migration to Flee from Persecution

☙ A DUTY OF BOTH MEN AND WOMEN:

God says in the Qur'an: "To those whom the angels gather in death while they are still wronging themselves, the angels will say: 'What were you doing?' They will answer: 'We were oppressed on earth.' (The angels) will say: 'Was not God's earth so spacious that you might have migrated to settle elsewhere?' Such will have their abode in Hell, a certainly evil end. Excepted are the men, women and children who, being truly helpless, can devise nothing and can find no way. These God may well pardon, then, for God is indeed Most Lenient, Much-Forgiving. Anyone who migrates for God's cause will find on earth many places for refuge and great abundance. He who leaves his home, fleeing from evil unto God and His Messenger, and is then overtaken by death, his reward is reserved for him with God. God is Much-Forgiving, Ever Merciful." (4: 97–100) Al-Zayn ibn al-Munīr says that these verses indicate that not only are women weak but that men can be just as weak.

☙ THE WEAKER ELEMENTS AND MIGRATION

God says in the Qur'an: "And why should you not fight in the cause of God and the utterly helpless men, women and children who are crying, 'Our Lord! Deliver us from this land whose people are oppressors, and send forth to us, out of Your grace, a protector, and send us one that will help us.'" (4: 75)

Migration to Abyssinia

'Ā'ishah narrated that both Umm Ḥabībah bint Abu Sufyān and Umm Salamah spoke about a church they saw in Abyssinia in which there were some statues. They mentioned this to the Prophet and he said: "Those people used to build a temple over the grave of a pious person and would put such statues in it. These will on the Day of Judgement be the worst of creatures in God's sight." (Related by al-Bukhari)

Abu Mūsā reports: "Asmā' bint 'Umays visited Ḥafṣah, the Prophet's wife. Asmā' was one of those who migrated to Negus's land..." (Related by Muslim)

Umm Khālid was the daughter of Khālid Sa'īd ibn al-'Āṣ and Ḥumaynah bint Khalaf. She reports: "I returned from Abyssinia [i.e. with her parents] and I was a young woman. The Prophet gave me a gift: a painted woollen dress. The Prophet rubbed the pattern with his hand and said: it is fine! It is fine!" (Related by al-Bukhari)

Ibn Ḥajar says: The women who joined the first migration to Abyssinia were Ruqayyah, the Prophet's daughter, Sahlah bint Suhayl who was Abu Hudhayfah's wife, Umm Salamah bint Abu Umayyah, Laylā bint Abu Ḥathamah who was 'Āmir ibn Rabī'ah's wife. Those who were in the second batch of migrants numbered 18 women, including Umm Ḥabībah bint Abu Sufyān, Asmā' bint 'Umays and Ḥumaynah bint Khalaf of the Khuzā'ah tribe.

Migration to Madinah

God says in the Qur'an: "Prophet! We have made lawful to you the wives whom you have paid their dowries, as well as those whom God has placed in your right hand through war, as also the daughters of your paternal uncles and aunts, and the daughters of your maternal uncles and aunts, who have migrated with you." (33: 50)

Asmā' bint Abu Bakr reports that she was pregnant with her first son 'Abdullāh ibn al-Zubayr. She said: "I set out almost on full term, going to Madinah. I stopped at Qubā' where I gave birth." (Related by al-Bukhari and Muslim)

Speaking of the Prophet's companions, Marwān and al-Miswar ibn Makhramah report: "When the Prophet entered into the peace agreement with Suhayl ibn 'Amr at al-Hudaybiyah, one of the conditions Suhayl stipulated in the agreement was that the Prophet 'would return to the Quraysh anyone who came to join you from our people, even though he be a follower of your faith...' During that period of truce, the Prophet returned to them every man who came to him even though he was a Muslim. Some female believers also migrated. Umm Kulthūm bint 'Uqbah ibn Abi Mu'ayṭ was among those who joined the Prophet during this period. She was a young woman who had recently attained puberty. Her people went to Madinah requesting that the Prophet return her, but he refused their request." (Related by al-Bukhari)

Abu Mūsā narrated: "We heard of the Prophet's migration to Madinah when we were in Yemen. We left to join him... Our boat landed us at Negus's land in Abyssinia where we met Ja'far ibn Abu Ṭālib and we stayed with him until we all went together to Madinah... Asmā' bint 'Umays, who came with us, visited Ḥafṣah..." (Related by al-Bukhari and Muslim)

'Ā'ishah narrated: "A black slave girl was set free by some Arabs, and she stayed with them. One day one of their girls went out wearing over her clothes a red strip of cloth adorned with jewels. She either put it down or dropped it. A small kite flew over and thought it to be meat. It picked it up and flew away. The girl's people looked for it but could not find it. They accused the slave girl of stealing it. They looked for it everywhere, and searched her even through her underwear. She said: 'I was standing there in their midst when the kite came over again and dropped the strip. It fell in between them. I said to them: You have accused me of stealing it, and here it is. I am totally innocent.' She went to the Prophet and embraced Islam. She had a small tent in the mosque where she stayed. She used to come to me and chat. Whenever she visited me she said this line of poetry: 'That day of the strip was a marvel from God. It is He Who has saved me from the land of disbelief.' I said to her: 'What is this thing about the strip that you mention whenever you come to me?' She told me this story." (Related by al-Bukhari)

Ibn Ḥajar says: "This hadith makes clear that it is appropriate to migrate from a town where a person has endured testing times. Indeed, he may be able to migrate to a better place, as happened to this young woman. It also shows the benefit of migrating from a place where the people are unbelievers."

In books of the Prophet's history and in biographies of his companions we read about migration by a number of women including al-'Abbās's wife, Umm al-Faḍl, Umm Salamah bint Abu Umayyah, Laylā bint Abu Ḥathamah, Umaymah bint 'Abd al-Muṭṭalib, Zaynab bint Jaḥsh, Ḥamnah bint Jaḥsh, Umm Ḥabībah bint Abu Sufyān, Judāmah bint Jandal, Umm Qays bint Miḥṣan, Umm Ḥabībah bint Nabātah, Umāmah bint Ruqaysh, Ḥafṣah bint 'Umar, Fāṭimah bint Qays, Subay'ah al-Aslamiyyah and Umm Rūmān. Al-Zuhrī says: "We do not know of any woman who migrated then renounced Islam after having accepted it." (Related by al-Bukhari)

Calling One's Community to Islam

'Imrān ibn Ḥuṣayn narrated: "We were travelling with the Prophet... We were extremely thirsty. As we walked on, we met a woman on her mount, with her two legs dropped between two large waterskins. We asked her where we could find water. She said: 'There is no water to be found here.' We asked: 'How far away from your people's quarters is the water spring?' She said: 'A day and a night's walk.' We said: 'Come with us to God's Messenger'... He ordered that the two waterskins be brought down... We filled every waterskin we had and every small leather container, but we did not give a drink to any of our camels.[22] Yet her waterskins were almost flowing with water. The Prophet then said to us: 'Bring what you can give her.' We brought her as much bread and dates as we could. She then went to her people. She said to them: 'I have just been with the most clever of all sorcerers, or perhaps he is a Prophet as they claim.' Her people were able to see the truth by what she told them. She and they soon embraced Islam." (Related by al-Bukhari and Muslim) Another version of this hadith adds: "The Muslims subsequently used to send expeditions against neighbouring idolater tribes, but they avoided that woman's people. One day she said to her people: 'It seems to me that these people are deliberately avoiding you. I suggest that we all accept Islam.' They accepted her advice and became Muslims." (Related by al-Bukhari and Muslim)

Many years before this woman embraced Islam and called on her people to do the same, another woman from the Quraysh in Makkah called Umm Sharīk embraced the new faith when Muslims were only a small, weak minority. She nevertheless used to visit other Qurayshī women, explain the message of Islam to them and call on them to accept Islam. When the people of Makkah realized what she was doing, they warned her, saying: "Had it not been for our respect of your people, we would have punished you severely."

Two: In the Muslim State

Women's Pledges to the Prophet

God gives the following instruction to the Prophet in the Qur'an: "Prophet! When believing women come and pledge to you that

---

22. Camels retain a large quantity of water in their bodies. Thus, they are able to travel long distances without having to drink. Hence, the Prophet did not use the woman's water for the camels, because it would have been unnecessary.

they will not associate any partner with God, nor steal, nor commit adultery, nor kill their children, nor lie about who fathered their children, nor disobey you in anything reasonable, then accept their pledge of allegiance and pray to God to forgive them. God is Much Forgiving, Ever Merciful." (60: 12)

'Abdullāh ibn 'Abbās narrated: "I attended the Eid al-Fiṭr Prayer with the Prophet, then with Abu Bakr and 'Uthmān. They all offered the prayer before the sermon and delivered the sermon after praying. The Prophet came down. I can almost see him now seating the men with his hand. Then he went through their ranks up to the women's rows and Bilāl was with him. He recited to them the verse that says: 'Prophet! When believing women come and pledge to you that they will not associate any partner with God, nor steal, nor commit adultery, nor kill their children, nor lie about who fathered their children,' he read the complete verse, then he asked them: 'Do you accept all these terms?' Only one woman answered him, saying: 'Yes, messenger of God!'[23] – Al-Ḥasan did not know who the woman was. – He said to them: 'Then, give what you can to charity.' Bilāl spread a robe and the women threw in it rings and larger pieces of jewellery." (Related by al-Bukhari and Muslim)

The fact that women pledged their allegiance to the Prophet is significant on more counts than one. It firstly indicated that a woman was fully independent; she was in no way a mere extension of a man. She gave her own pledge of allegiance in the same way as a man. Secondly, the pledge given by women is the normal pledge to be a Muslim and to obey God's Messenger. In this pledge, men and women are alike. Men sometimes gave their pledges to the Prophet in the same terms as women. 'Ubādah ibn al-Ṣāmit narrated: "God's

23. The others indicated their agreement by remaining silent, which was normal practice of women at the time. This is indicated by their response to the Prophet's call for charitable donations.

Messenger said to a group of his companions: 'Come and pledge to me that you will not associate any partner with God, nor steal, nor commit adultery, nor kill your children, nor lie about who fathered your children, nor disobey me in anything reasonable.' I gave him my pledge in these terms." (Related by al-Bukhari) There is an additional pledge only men give, which is the pledge to join the jihad campaigns and to ensure the Prophet's protection. The pledge given by the Prophet's companions on the Day of al-Hudaybiyah, known as al-Riḍwān Pledge, was of this special type.

Thirdly, women's pledges to the Prophet are based on two important facts: that he is the one who delivers God's message to mankind and that he is the leader of the Muslim community. This second fact is emphasised by the last of the terms of the pledge, 'nor disobey you in anything reasonable'. In reference to obedience due to rulers, the Prophet says: "Obedience applies only to what is reasonable."

That women gave these pledges to the Prophet reminds us of the fact that some women attended the second pledge given by the Anṣār to the Prophet at al-ʿAqabah alongside the men. In an authentic hadith, Kaʿb ibn Mālik reports: "We went out on pilgrimage together with some idolaters of our own people. We had already been praying and we had learnt what our new faith required. Among us was al-Barā' ibn Maʿrūr, our chief and elder man... We met at al-ʿAqabah: seventy-three men and two women, Umm ʿImārah bint Kaʿb from the Māzin clan and Asmā' bint ʿAmr ibn ʿAdiy, a woman from the Salamah clan..."

Testing Migrant Women

God says in the Qur'an: "Believers! When believing women come to you as migrants, test them. God knows best their faith. If you ascertain that they are believers, do not send them back to the unbelievers. They are no longer lawful [as wives] for the unbelievers, and these are no longer lawful to them." (60:10)

Al-Miswar ibn Makhramah and Marwān narrate, each confirming the other's report: "The Prophet travelled at the time of al-Hudaybiyah... Suhayl ibn ʿAmr came over. He said: 'Come let us write down the terms of agreement between us.' The Prophet called in a scribe and told him to write... Then Suhayl added: 'If any man from among us comes to you, you shall return him to us even though he may be a follower of your faith... Then some women came over declaring their belief. God then revealed the verse that begins with: 'Believers! When believing women come to you as migrants, test them.'" (Related by al-Bukhari) Ibn Ḥajar comments: "Among the women this statement refers to were Umaymah bint Bishr, Ḥassān ibn Daḥdāḥah's wife... Subayʿah bint al-Ḥārith, Musāfir al-Makhzūmī's wife... Burūgh bint ʿUqbah, Shammās ibn ʿUthmān's wife... and ʿAbdah bint ʿAbd al-ʿAzīz ibn Naḍlah, ʿAmr ibn ʿAbd Wadd's wife."

ʿĀ'ishah narrated: "When women came over to the Prophet, having migrated to join him, he would test them in accordance with the verse that begins with: 'Believers! When believing women come to you as migrants, test them.' Whoever of them accepted this condition had to take the test." (Related by al-Bukhari) Ibn Ḥajar says in his commentary that the last sentence in the hadith refers to the condition of faith. A clearer statement is the hadith related by al-Ṭabarī on Ibn ʿAbbās's authority: "Their test required them to declare their belief that there is no deity other than God and that Muhammad is His Messenger." In another report, also by al-Ṭabarī on Ibn ʿAbbās's authority, was that a woman had to solemnly declare: "By God, I have not come out of any hate I harbour towards any husband; by God, I have not come merely to move from one land to another; by God, I have not come seeking any gain; by God, I have only come here motivated by my love for God and His Messenger."

Encouraging a Suitor to Believe

Jābir ibn ʿAbdullāh quotes the Prophet as saying: "I was shown heaven and I saw there Abu Ṭalḥah's wife." (Related by Muslim) Abu

Ṭalḥah's wife was Umm Sulaym. The story of their marriage shows that she was a woman of great confidence, assured in her faith, keen to present it to her suitor. She first invited him to accept her new faith. Ibn Sa'd relates in his *al-Ṭabaqāt*, "When Abu Ṭalḥah proposed to Umm Sulaym, she said to him: 'Abu Ṭalḥah! Do you not know that the deity you worship is no more than a tree that comes out of the earth, and that was planted by an Abyssinian farmhand? Do you not know that these deities your people worship... would burn if you set fire to them?... Are you not aware that the stone you worship cannot cause you either harm or benefit?...'"

Thābit al-Bunānī quotes Anas as saying: "Abu Ṭalḥah proposed marriage to Umm Sulaym. She said to him: 'You are certainly a man who would not be rejected by anyone, but you are an unbeliever and I am a Muslim. It is not lawful for me to marry you. If you would accept Islam, I will take that as my dowry and will ask nothing else.' [It should be remembered that he was perhaps the richest man in Madinah.] Abu Ṭalḥah accepted Islam, and that was the dowry she received." Thābit al-Bunānī comments: "I never heard of a woman who had a more precious dowry than Umm Sulaym. Hers was Islam." (Related by al-Nasā'ī) This took place at the time when Islam was just establishing itself in Madinah. Its roots then were not firmly established and Madinah was a city where Muslims lived alongside idolaters and Jews.

Women's Participation in Defending Islam

Al-Rubayyi' bint Mu'awwidh reports: "We used to go on jihad campaigns with the Prophet. We would provide drinks and serve the people, nurse the wounded and remove the casualties, whether wounded or killed, to Madinah." (Related by al-Bukhari)

Anas ibn Mālik reports: "... The Prophet said: 'I have been shown some of my followers going on an expedition to serve God's cause, riding on the sea and looking like kings on their couches.' Umm Ḥarām said: 'Messenger of God! Please pray to God to make me one of them.' He prayed for her..." (Related by al-Bukhari and Muslim)

Here we have only cited these two hadiths on women's participation in jihad. Others can be found in those chapters dealing with women's role in the Muslim community's social life.

A Woman's Declaration of Allegiance

'Ā'ishah narrated that Hind bint 'Utbah said to the Prophet: "Messenger of God! There were times when there were no people on earth I would have loved to see more humiliated than your people. Today, there are no people on earth I love to see honoured more than your people." (Related by al-Bukhari and Muslim)

Honouring a Woman's Pledge of Protection

Umm Hāni' bint Abu Ṭālib narrated: "I went to see the Prophet after Makkah had fallen to Islam. I found him taking a bath and Fāṭimah, his daughter, was screening him. I said my greeting to him. He asked: 'Who is this?' I said that I was Umm Hāni' bint Abu Ṭālib. He welcomed me. When he finished his ablutions, he stood up and offered a prayer of eight short *rak'ahs* wearing only one garment. I then said to him: 'Messenger of God! My brother, 'Alī, says that he would kill a man to whom I extended protection. The man is Habīrah's son.' The Prophet said: 'We will honour your pledge of protection.'" (Related by al-Bukhari and Muslim)

Women Taking Interest in Political Affairs

Umm Salamah Responds to a General Call:

'Abdullāh ibn Rāfi' narrated: "Umm Salamah, the Prophet's wife, used to tell people: 'I was being combed when I heard the Prophet standing on the platform and saying: "You, people."' She said to the woman combing her: 'Tie up my hair.'" (Related by Muslim) In another version that directly quotes Umm Salamah: "I said to the woman: 'Hold off.' She said: 'He only called on men to come, not women.' I said to her. 'I am one of the people.'" (Related by Muslim)

☙ Umm Salamah Interested in the Action against the Qurayẓah:

Usāmah ibn Zayd narrated that the Angel Gabriel visited the Prophet when Umm Salamah was with him. They talked, then he departed. The Prophet said to Umm Salamah: 'Who was this?' She said: 'This is Diḥyah.'[24] Umm Salamah said: 'By God, I thought him none other than Diḥyah until I heard the Prophet's speech reporting what Gabriel said.' (Related by al-Bukhari and Muslim)

This report of Umm Salamah is given in a very short version. 'Ā'ishah clarifies what the Angel Gabriel said to the Prophet, which he subsequently mentioned in his speech to the people. 'Ā'ishah said: "Gabriel came to him (after he had returned from the Battle of the Moat) and said: 'You have laid down your arms! We certainly have not. Go out to them.' The Prophet asked: 'To whom?' He said: 'This way.' He pointed towards the Qurayẓah quarters." (Related by al-Bukhari)

☙ Fāṭimah bint Qays Attends a Public Meeting

Fāṭimah bint Qays reports: "After I had finished my waiting period, I heard the Prophet's caller announcing, 'All come to prayer,'[25] and I went to the mosque and offered the prayer with the Prophet. I was in the women's row that was immediately to the men's back.

---

24. Sometimes Gabriel took the form of Diḥyah ibn Khalīfah, a companion of the Prophet.
25. This was how public meetings were announced. The caller would go around and make this call and the people would then flock to the mosque where there would be a short prayer before the Prophet made whatever announcement he wanted to make.

[Another version describes her position in this way: I was in the first women's row which was just next to the men's rows.] When the Prophet finished his prayer, he sat on the platform, smiling. He said: 'Let everyone stay where they have prayed.' He then asked: 'Do you know why I have asked you to come to this meeting?' They said: 'God and His Messenger know best.' He said: 'I have not gathered you to give you any pleasant or unpleasant news...' (Related by Muslim)

☙ Future Worries:

Qays ibn Abi Hazim reports: "Abu Bakr was at the place of a woman from the Aḥmus tribe called Zaynab bint al-Muhājir when he noticed that she did not speak. He asked why she did not speak, and he was told that she had pledged to offer the pilgrimage uttering no word throughout her journey. He said to her: 'Speak, for such a pledge is unlawful. It is a practice people used to do in the days of ignorance.' She started to speak, and she asked him who he was. He said: 'I am one of the Muhājirīn.' She asked: 'Which of them?' He said: 'I am from the Quraysh.' She again asked: 'Which clan of the Quraysh?' He said: 'You certainly ask. I am Abu Bakr.' She asked: 'How long will we maintain this good code which God has granted us after we were in ignorance?' He said: 'You will maintain it as long as your leaders maintain the right way.' She asked: 'What leaders?' He said: 'Do your people not have notable figures who will be obeyed when they give an order?' She said: 'Indeed.' He said: 'These are the ones I mean.'" (Related by al-Bukhari)

☙ 'Ā'ishah Enquires after a Leader's Conduct

'Abd al-Raḥmān ibn Shammās reports: "I went to 'Ā'ishah with a question. She asked me: 'Who are you?' I said: 'I am a man from Egypt.' She asked: 'How was your leader's conduct with you during your last expedition?' I said: 'We had nothing to complain of. If any of us suffered the death of a camel or a slave, he would give him a camel or a slave in place of what he lost. When anyone needed money, he would give him some money'..." (Related by Muslim)

Giving Advice on Political Matters

☙ Umm Salamah Advises the Prophet:

Al-Miswar ibn Makhramah and Marwān report, each confirming the other's report: "The Prophet travelled at the time of al-Ḥudaybiyah... Suhayl ibn ʿAmr came over. He said: 'Come let us write down the terms of agreement between us.' The Prophet called in a scribe and told him to write *Bismillāh al-Raḥmān al-Raḥīm*, [which means: 'In the name of God, the Lord of Grace, the Ever Merciful']. Suhayl said: 'I certainly do not know what this, al-Raḥmān, is. Write as you used to: *Bismik Allahumm* [or in God's name].' The Muslims said: 'By God, we shall not write anything other than *Bismillāh al-Raḥmān al-Raḥīm*.' The Prophet told the scribe to write what Suhayl wanted... Then the Prophet said to him: 'On condition that you shall give us free access to the Kaʿbah to do our worship.' Suhayl said: 'No one in Arabia shall say that we have succumbed to force. This we agree to take place next year.' These terms were written down. Suhayl said: 'Another condition is that if any man from among us comes to you, even though he follows your faith, you shall return him to us.' The Muslims said: 'Limitless is God in His glory. How is he to be returned when he has come to us a Muslim?'... ʿUmar ibn al-Khaṭṭāb said: 'I went to the Prophet and said: Are you not truly God's Prophet?' He said: "Yes, indeed." I asked again: Are we not following the truth and our enemies following falsehood? He said: "Yes." I said: Why then do we accept humiliation on account of our faith? He said: "I am God's Messenger. I will never disobey Him and He will grant me support."[26] I still asked: Did you not tell us that we would visit the Kaʿbah and do the walk around it? He said: "Yes,

26. This is a clear indication that the Prophet was acting on God's orders. This is the reason why he did not consult any of his companions regarding making this peace deal with the idolaters who had been fighting him ever since he migrated to Madinah six years earlier, and had been persecuting the Muslims long before that.

but did I tell you that you would do it this year?" I said that he did not. He said: "Then, you shall visit it and do the walk around it"'... When the terms of the peace agreement had been written down, the Prophet said to his companions: 'Now slaughter your sacrifices and shave your heads.'[27] By God, not a single man of them did so, even though he said it three times. When he felt their lack of response, he went into his tent and told his wife, Umm Salamah, of people's attitude. She said to him: 'Prophet, do you like that they should do as you told them? Go out yourself and without speaking to any of them slaughter your sacrifice and call on someone to shave your head.' He did just that: he slaughtered his sacrifice and asked someone who shaved his head. When they saw him doing this, they all rose and did the same, with some shaving their friends' heads." (Related by al-Bukhari)

Umm Sulaym Gives Advice:

Anas ibn Mālik reports that his mother, Umm Sulaym, said to the Prophet... on the day of the Battle of Ḥunayn... "Messenger of God! Kill those people whom you had set free because they deserted you." He said: "Umm Sulaym. God's support is enough for us, and He has given us much."[28] (Related by Muslim)

---

27. The Prophet and his companions had already started their worship ritual, the 'umrah, shortly after setting out from Madinah, and had travelled more than 400 kilometres in the state of consecration which they were required to maintain until they had completed their rituals at the Ka'bah. These rituals are completed by the slaughter of their sacrifices and shaving their heads, or cutting some of their hair short. When the Prophet ordered them to do this at their place of encampment, it signalled that they were not to continue their trip into Makkah and that they would return without offering their rituals. This was hard for them to accept. Hence, their reluctance to act on the Prophet's order. Umm Salamah's advice aimed to deal with their lack of response.
28. Those were the people of Makkah. At the time Makkah fell to Islam, they all surrendered. The Prophet granted them their freedom and did not punish them. Many of them accepted Islam then, but they were still newcomers, not firm in their belief. Hence, Umm Sulaym thought them to be hypocrites and that they deserved to be killed for their desertion in battle. – Author's note.

☙ Ḥafṣah's Advice to Her Brother

1. ʿAbdullāh ibn ʿUmar narrated: "I went to see Ḥafṣah and she said to me: 'Have you heard that your father is not appointing a successor?' I said: 'He would not do that.' She said: 'Yes, indeed, he is doing that.' I swore that I would take it up with him. Yet I kept quiet till the next day without speaking to him about it. I felt like I was carrying a mountain on my shoulders. I went back to him and he asked me about the situation among the people. I said: I heard people saying something and I resolved to take it up with you. They allege that you are not appointing a successor. May I say that if you had a shepherd looking after your camels or your sheep and he left your flock and came to you, you would hold him to be negligent of his duty. Looking after the community is much more serious. He reflected on what I said for a while, then, lifting his head, he said to me: 'God will certainly look after His faith. If I do not appoint a successor, God's Messenger did not appoint a successor. If I do, Abu Bakr did.' By God, when he mentioned the Prophet and Abu Bakr, I realised that he would never follow anyone other than the Prophet and that he would not appoint a successor." (Related by Muslim)

2. Abdullah ibn ʿUmar narrated: "I went to see Hafsah and saw her hair dripping. I said to her: You know how the situation in the Muslim community has developed but I have not been invited. She said: 'Go and join them. They are waiting for you, and I fear that if you stay away, disunity may still persist.'" She continued to press him until he went to join them. (Related by al-Bukhari) Ibn Ḥajar comments that ʿAbdullāh ibn ʿUmar's remark concerning developments in the Muslim community refers to the fighting that took place between ʿAlī and Muʿāwiyah in the Battle of Ṣiffīn and their eventual agreement on arbitration to sort out their differences... They had agreed a time to meet and look at the

situation. Ibn ʿUmar consulted his sister, Ḥafṣah, on joining the arbitrators. She advised him to attend, fearing that his absence might lead to the dispute remaining unresolved... One report mentioned by ʿAbd al-Razzāq with a good chain of transmission quotes ʿAbdullāh ibn ʿUmar as saying: "On the day when Muʿāwiyah held the meeting at Dūmat al-Jandal, Ḥafṣah said to me: 'It is not right that you should stay away from a meeting that aims to achieve reconciliation within the Muslim community when you are the Prophet's brother-in-law and ʿUmar ibn al-Khaṭṭāb's son.'"

Increasing Awareness of the Prophet's Guidance in Politics

Umm Salamah narrated that God's Messenger (peace be upon him) said: "You will have some leaders who will do certain things that are acceptable and others that are not. Whoever dislikes what is unacceptable is free of blame and whoever speaks out against it is safe. It is only those who accept the unacceptable and toe the line that are party to it. People asked: 'Should we fight them, Messenger of God?' He said: 'No, as long as they continue to offer their prayers.'" (Related by Muslim)

ʿAbd al-Raḥmān ibn Shammās reports that he went to ʿĀ'ishah asking her about something. She said to me: "I will tell you what I heard God's Messenger say in this home of mine: 'My Lord! Whoever is in charge of some of my followers' affairs and is hard on them, be hard on him; and whoever is in charge of some of their affairs and is kind to them, be kind to him.'" (Related by Muslim)

Yaḥyā ibn Ḥuṣayn reports hearing his grandmother, Umm al-Ḥuṣayn, saying: "I joined God's Messenger on his Farewell Pilgrimage. The Prophet made a long speech, and then I heard him say: 'If a slave whose ear or nose has been cut off – and I think she added 'black' – becomes your ruler and he conducts your affairs following God's Book, then listen to him and obey him.'" (Related by Muslim)

ʿUbaydillāh ibn al-Qibṭiyyah reports that he was with al-Ḥārith ibn Abi Rabīʿah and ʿAbdullāh ibn Ṣafwān when they visited Umm Salamah, the Prophet's wife. They asked her about the army that will be swallowed by the earth. She told them that the Prophet said: "Someone will seek shelter in the Kaʿbah, and an army is sent against him. As the army will be traversing a barren stretch of land, they will be swallowed by the earth." She added: "I asked him what happens to one in the army who is opposed to their mission?" He said: "He will be swallowed with them, but on the Day of Judgement he will be treated according to his intentions." (Related by Muslim)

Women in Opposition to Muslim Rulers

ʿĀ'ishah's Role during ʿAlī's Reign:

ʿAbdullāh ibn Ziyād al-Asadī reports: "When Ṭalḥah, al-Zubayr and ʿĀ'ishah travelled to Basrah, ʿAlī sent ʿAmmār ibn Yāsir and Ḥasan ibn ʿAlī. They came to us at Kufah. Al-Ḥasan stood up on the platform and ʿAmmār stood lower than him. We gathered there. I heard ʿAmmār saying: "ʿĀ'ishah has gone to Basrah and I certainly know that she is the Prophet's wife both in this life and the next, but God is testing you so that He knows whether you obey him or her.'" (Related by al-Bukhari)

This case demonstrates that a woman could stand in opposition to a Muslim ruler. In this hadith, ʿAmmār does not deny that ʿĀ'ishah had the right to express her views or to demand as she did - together with some of the most honoured companions of the Prophet - that ʿUthmān's killers should be punished. He was however, critical of her march with such a large host as that might lead to a flaring up between two Muslim groups. ʿAmmār's attitude was in turn criticised by Abu Mūsā and Abu Masʿūd as they viewed it as part of the preparations to fight the other group. Abu Wā'il reports: "Abu Mūsā and Abu Masʿūd went to ʿAmmār when ʿAlī sent him to raise support in Kufah. They said to him: 'Ever since you became a Muslim, we have not seen you doing something we disliked more than the effort you are putting into this affair.' He replied: 'For my part, I have not seen the two of you, ever since you became Muslim, doing something I disliked more than your staying away from this affair.'" (Related by al-Bukhari)

Abu Bakarah was critical of both parties, the ruler's supporters and the opposition, for their hardened attitudes. Al-Aḥnaf ibn Qays reports: "I went out fully armed during the period of strife. I met Abu Bakarah and he asked me where I was going. I said: 'To support the Prophet's cousin.' He told me that the Prophet said: 'If two Muslims cross arms, then both the killer and the killed will be in hell.' People asked him: 'We understand about the killer, but why the one who is killed?' He said: 'Because he intended to kill his opponent.'" (Related by al-Bukhari) Abu Bakarah himself reports: "During the days leading to the Battle of the Camel, I benefitted by a word I heard: when the Prophet was told that the Persian Empire appointed Khosrow's daughter as their ruler, he said: 'People who assign their affairs to a woman shall not be successful.'" (Related by al-Bukhari)

Reporting on these historical events has not been easy for us, because they involved fighting between two groups of Muslims, both of whom were honourable and commanding great respect by all believers. Nonetheless we have overcome our reluctance in order to present a full picture of women's positions and roles, as we have promised.

Asmā' and Her Role during al-Ḥajjāj's Time:

Abu Nawfal reports:[29] "I saw 'Abdullāh ibn al-Zubayr's body hung at the entrance to Makkah. The people of the Quraysh and others

29. The report that follows speaks of the aftermath of the battle between 'Abdullāh ibn al-Zubayr, who claimed the caliphate and was at one stage in control of Arabia and Iraq, and al-Ḥajjāj ibn Yūsuf, the commander of the army sent by the Umayyad Caliph 'Abd al-Malik ibn Marwān to subdue him. The battle took place in Makkah and ended when 'Abdullāh ibn al-Zubayr was killed.

passed by until ʿAbdullāh ibn ʿUmar stood there and addressed him: 'Peace be to you, Abu Khubayb. [He repeated this three times.] I certainly counselled you not to go on this course. [Again he repeated this three times.] By God, you were, to the best of my knowledge, a man of piety, frequently fasting and doing night worship, and kind to your kinsfolk. If you are counted as the worst person in a community, then that is a community of good people.' ʿAbdullāh ibn ʿUmar then moved on. What he did and said was reported to al-Ḥajjāj. He sent soldiers who took the body down and buried it within the graves of the Jews.[30] Al-Ḥajjāj then sent to his [Ibn al-Zubayr's] mother, Asmā' bint Abu Bakr, asking her to come to him. She refused. He sent his messenger again with the message, 'You shall come to me or I will send someone to drag you here by your hair.' She again refused, telling the messenger to tell him: 'By God, I shall not come to you even though you send someone to drag me by my hair.' When he was told this, he said: 'Give me my shoes.' He went out feeling triumphant. When he arrived at her place, he asked her: 'What do you think of what I did with God's enemy?' She said: 'You have ruined this present life for him while he ruined your future life for you. I am told that you refer to him as the son of the woman with two girdles. I am that woman. I used one to tie up the food for the Prophet and Abu Bakr and cover it, and the other was the one no woman can do without. God's Messenger told us that from the tribe of Thaqīf, there will come a liar and a destroyer. We have certainly seen the liar.[31] As for the destroyer, I feel that you are the one.' He left her without saying a word." (Related by Muslim)

---

30. This is problematic. No Jews lived in Makkah prior to Islam or in its early period. Some Jews, like Kaʿb ibn al-Ashraf and Ḥuyay ibn Akhtab, visited Makkah on some occasions, but none is reported to have died there. Nor was there any Jewish tribe living in the vicinity of Makkah at any time. Although the report is authentic, as it is related in one of the two authentic hadith anthologies, this sentence might have been introduced at a later stage.
31. Asmā' was able to put things into the proper perspective. When al-Ḥajjāj referred to her son as 'God's enemy' she told him that by killing her son, he

Here we see how a woman stood firm against a tyrannical governor, who was revelling at his triumph, betraying no sense of fear. On the contrary, she rebuked him with stinging words and left him speechless.

We conclude with the case of the Queen of Sheba as mentioned in the Qur'an. She was a queen of immense intelligence and wisdom, following in her rule a course based on consultation. She ultimately accepted the faith based on total submission to God, the Lord of all the worlds. Thus, the Qur'an tells us that a woman can be far wiser than most men in conducting her people's affairs. As told in the Qur'an, the story begins when Solomon was inspecting the birds:

> He inspected the birds and said: "Why is it that I do not see the hoopoe? Is he among the absentees? I will certainly punish him severely or I will kill him unless He brings me a clear warrant [for his absence]." But the hoopoe did not take long in coming. He said: "I have just learnt things that are unknown to you and I come to you from Sheba with accurate information. I found there a woman ruling over them; and she has been given of all good things, and hers is a magnificent throne. I found her and her people prostrating themselves to the sun instead of God; and Satan has made their deeds seem goodly to them, thus turning them away from the path [of God], so that they cannot find the right way. That they should not prostrate

---

spoilt his life on earth, while he was yet to account to God for killing him. The point she mentions about her girdles refers to the time the Prophet and her father, Abu Bakr, migrated to Madinah. She went to their hiding place to take food for them. One the day they were to start their journey, she forgot to wrap the food up, so she tore her girdle in two, using one part to wrap the food and the other to hold her clothes in place. The reference to the liar from the Thaqīf tribe points to al-Mukhtār ibn 'Ubaydillāh who claimed himself a prophet. Al-Ḥajjāj belonged to the same tribe.

themselves in worship of God who brings forth all that is hidden in the heavens and the earth, and knows what you conceal and what you reveal. God, other than whom there is no deity, the Lord of the [truly] magnificent Throne."

Said [Solomon]: "We shall see whether you have told the truth or you are a liar. Go with this my letter and deliver it to them; and then draw back from them, and see what answer they return." [The Queen of Sheba] said: "Know, my nobles, that a worthy letter has been delivered to me. It is from Solomon, and it reads, 'In the name of God, the Lord of Grace, the Ever Merciful: Do not exalt yourselves against me, but come to me in submission [to God].' Nobles, counsel me in this my affair; no decision on any matter do I take unless you are present." They said: "We are endowed with power and with mighty prowess in war; but the command is yours. Consider, then, what you would command." Said she: "When kings enter a country, they despoil it, and make the noble ones of its people the most abject. Thus do they behave. Hence, I am going to send these people a gift and wait to see what the envoys bring back."

When [the Queen's envoy] came to Solomon, he said: "Is it gold that you would give me? What God has given me is much better than all that He has given you. Yet you rejoice with your own gift. Go back to them, for we shall certainly come to them with forces they cannot match, and we shall certainly drive them from the land in disgrace, and they will be utterly humbled." Solomon said: "Which of you nobles can bring me her throne before they come to me in submission?" Said an afreet of the jinn: "I shall bring it to you before you rise from your position. I am powerful enough to do it, and worthy of trust." But the one who was deeply versed in the Book said: "I shall bring it to you within the twinkling of your eye." When he saw it standing before him, he said: "This is by the grace of my Lord, so as to test me whether I am grateful or ungrateful. He who is grateful [to God] is but grateful for his own good. As for him who is ungrateful... My Lord is self-sufficient, most generous." He [then] said: "Alter the appearance of her throne: let us see whether she will be able to recognize it, or she will remain unguided."

So when she arrived, she was asked: "Is your throne like this?" She answered: "It looks as though it were the same. We were endowed with knowledge before her, and we have surrendered ourselves." Yet that which she used to worship instead of God had kept her away [from the true faith]. She belonged to an unbelieving nation. She was told to enter the court. When she saw it, she thought it was a lake of water, and she bared her legs. Said he: "It is but a court smoothly paved with glass!" She said: "My Lord! I have indeed wronged my soul, but now I submit myself, with Solomon, to God, the Lord of all the worlds." (27: 20–44)

Social Aspects Relevant to Women's Political Activity in Contemporary Society

1. Colonialism swept most areas of the Muslim world followed by the creation of the Zionist state in Palestine. This has practically imposed that women should participate in the struggle for independence, i.e. jihad. Women have contributed much to liberation movements in many Muslim countries.
2. Social interaction with easier means of transportation and greater media coverage has led to greater political awareness among men and women, as well as better and easier monitoring of and participation in politics.

3. Better, varied and specialised education available to boys and girls at all stages, together with more women going out to work and participating in social activity has enabled more women to take part in political activity, including demonstrations, voting in elections at all levels, contesting elections and joining political parties, national fronts and organisations.
4. More complex human society giving women a more complex life has led to the emergence of new problems and new issues in women's lives. Hence, the need for women to be more active in local and legislative counsels to give greater insight into these issues and play a more active role in finding solutions for them.
5. Broader consultation at the global level, even though its implementation varies from one place to another has encouraged governments in Arab and Muslim countries to take some steps to establish better consultation. Some of these initiatives have been serious whilst some lacked substance. Nevertheless, people everywhere, men and women, continue to aspire to greater consultation in politics, while all nationalist parties and organisations demand greater and more substantive consultation.

Contemporary Political Activity

1. Political activity includes efforts related to the way the legislative and executive authorities are formed and their respective remits and how they conduct their business. When individuals take an interest in political affairs, following events and studying issues, better awareness of what takes place and of the aims and objectives is achieved. All this enables people to positively contribute to political activity.
2. Social activity provides a natural platform from which to move into political activity. When people are socially active, they are better aware of the concerns of their community. While social activity consists of the role of individuals in such concerns,

political activity relates in greater measure to the government in power. The two roles are always interrelated.

3. The main aspects of political activity are:
    i. Real participation in choosing the overall ruler;
    ii. Participation in choosing the community's representatives in legislative counsels which have the dual functions of enacting laws and holding the Executive to account;
    iii. Voicing opinions, either in support of or in opposition to what the Executive and Legislative authorities adopt. This may be by speaking against them, writing articles, organising demonstrations, going on strike, signing petitions, etc.;
    iv. Taking part in activities organised by political parties or other nationalist forces, and
    v. Contesting elections for local and legislative counsels.

4. Political activity requires a greater measure of awareness and education and a wider scope of concerns. These qualities may at first be found in a small number of men and women, but their numbers are bound to increase in an atmosphere of public freedom and growing participation in politics. These two factors are vital if we are to enhance awareness among the population so that people can play their role in making the political authority benefit by society's collective wisdom. Men differ a great deal in their involvement in politics, according to their abilities and positions. The same applies to women among whom we find some who are unlettered and others who are highly educated, housewives spending most of their time at home and ones who pursue a wide range of activities both at home and outside. Some working women have limited responsibilities while others undertake wide responsibilities in a variety of fields such as medicine, education, and the dissemination of information, etc. Each such woman has her own unique ability to participate in political activity.

Principles Relating to Women's Political Activity in Contemporary Society

Principle One:

> Every Muslim woman is invited, in the same way as every Muslim man, to be interested in her community's political affairs and to contribute to the advancement of her community according to her ability, by enjoining what is right, forbidding what is wrong and giving sincere advice. In other words, by strengthening positive elements and resisting deviation. All this falls within jihad that earns reward from God, as its objective is to ensure just and wise government.

Nothing epitomises women's concerns about her society better than Umm Salamah's words: "I am one of the people." She made it clear that the ruler's call for people to assemble was addressed to men and women alike. Likewise, Fāṭimah bint Qays expressed the truth as she said: "I went to the mosque along with the people who went." She thus went with men in response to the ruler's call. (Both cases are given in detail under the examples of women's participation in politics in the land of Islam.)

As regards women's role in the progress of their community and ensuring just and wise government, God says in the Qur'an: "The believers, men and women, are friends to one another: They enjoin what is right and forbid what is wrong; they attend to their prayers, and pay their zakat, and obey God and His Messenger. It is on these that God will have mercy. Surely, God is Almighty, Wise." (9: 71)

Tamīm al-Dārī quotes the Prophet as saying: "'Religion is sincerity.' We said: To whom? He said: 'To God, His Book, His Messenger and to the leaders of the Muslims and their common folk.'" (Related by Muslim)

Jarīr ibn ʿAbdullāh reports: "... I said to the Prophet: I have come to pledge my loyalty as a believer in Islam. He made a condition that I should give sincere advice to all Muslims. I gave him my pledge in these terms..." (Related by al-Bukhari and Muslim)

Sincere counsel is given paramount position in the divine faith. The Prophet expresses this in his hadith reported by Tamīm al-Dārī as he defines religion as sincerity. The Prophet uses the term *naṣīḥah*, which has the primary meaning of giving good and sincere counsel. Indeed, true religion cannot be practised without such sincerity. Needless to say, religion belongs to every Muslim man and woman alike. We all, men and women, will be accountable to God for discharging this duty of giving sincere advice to both the leaders of the Muslims and their common folk. Everyone is required to do so according to his or her position and ability. Such sincerity has two aspects: an inner one, which is to wish all Muslims well whoever they might be, and a practical one which is to voice one's opinion and proclaim the truth, even though this may be hard or costly.

Commenting on the verse that begins with, "The believers, men and women, are friends to one another," Shaikh Rashīd Riḍā says: "... This verse makes it clear that it is a duty of all Muslims, men and women alike, to enjoin right and to forbid wrong. This includes verbal statements and written ones, as also criticising governors, be they caliphs, kings, presidents or their subordinates. Women used to be aware of this and practise it."[32] This is certainly true. Samrā' bint Nuhayk, as we have reported under social activity, used to implement this, standing up to those below the ranks of caliphs and governors, ordering them to abide by what is right and to refrain from what is wrong. Umm al-Dardā', a companion of the Prophet, objected to a caliph's action and corrected his behaviour when she found it unbecoming. Zayd ibn Aslam reports that the

32. M.R. Riḍā, *Nidā' ila al-Jins al-Laṭīf*, Al-Maktab al-Islami, Beirut, p. 13.

Caliph, 'Abd al-Malik ibn Marwān, sent to Umm al-Dardā' some articles of soft furniture he had. One day, 'Abd al-Malik was up at night and he called his servant to come over to him. When the servant was slow in coming, the caliph cursed him. In the morning, Umm al-Dardā' said to him: "I overheard you cursing your servant when you called him. I heard my husband quoting the Prophet as he said: 'Cursers will be neither intercessors nor witnesses on the Day of Judgement.'" (Related by Muslim)

Principle Two:

> Political activity may at times be a duty. Every Muslim woman should do what may be considered a collective duty for women in this respect.

Such collective duties include:

1. Every action that must be taken to ensure wise and just government and in which women's efforts are needed together with men's efforts so as to be properly accomplished. A good example is to elect the best candidates to national legislative bodies, municipal councils and trade union executives, as also taking part in referendums on public issues. They thus help to establish right and to outlaw wrong.
2. Joining political parties and groups that they deem to be sincere and working for the general good of the community and to ensure just government. These should be working for comprehensive reform based on Islamic principles on the one hand, and on human experience and contemporary knowledge on the other. They will, thus, be able to support sincere parties and groups in facing up to the forces hostile to Islam and to parties that work for their own gains.
3. Spreading political awareness among women, particularly in special periods such as the lead up to general elections. This may involve a collective duty for women, particularly when it

involves visits to people's homes and speaking to women and answering their questions.

4. Providing supervision of how elections are conducted so as to ensure objectivity and neutrality.

We mentioned earlier that our backward societies pay little attention to collective duties in the social field. Similar collective duties in the political field are even more grossly neglected, despite the very hard situations Muslims find themselves in as a result of external pressures, despotism and most people's lack of interest in public affairs. It is extremely important that men and women acquire better awareness so that they realize the seriousness of neglecting such duties and begin to exert efforts to see them fulfilled. Only in this way can they relieve themselves of accountability for their negligence and contribute to the progress of their communities. They would also earn generous reward from God in the life to come.

When the political situation in Muslim society is set on a proper course, ensuring wise and just leadership that is always willing to abide by the rules of Islamic law, political activity becomes recommended, rather than a duty, aiming to ensure further progress.

We would like to draw the attention of Muslim women to the fact that when they neglect their duty to be involved in political activity, even at the risk of occasional persecution, they leave the field open to other women to take their place. Such women may be motivated by personal greed or ambition or some other objective that is contrary to Islamic interests. They will join men of similar orientation in supporting forces that are hostile to Islam or those who may scheme against the Muslim community.

Muslim women must be fully aware of what hostile women did during the Prophet's lifetime. One woman used to place harmful objects on the Prophet's path, as is stated in the Qur'an: "Doomed are the hands of Abu Lahab; doomed is he. His wealth and his gains shall avail him nothing. He shall have to endure a flaming fire, and his wife, the carrier of firewood, shall have a rope of palm fibre round her neck." (111: 1-5) Another woman spoke sarcastically to the Prophet. Jundab ibn Sufyān reports: "The Prophet was ill, and he could not do his night worship for two or three nights. A woman came to him and said: 'Muhammad! I hope that your jinnee has abandoned you. I have not seen him coming near you for two or three nights.' God then revealed the surah starting with the verses: 'By the bright morning hours, and the night when it grows still and dark, your Lord has neither forsaken you, nor does He hate you.'" (93: 1-3) (Related by al-Bukhari and Muslim)

It is also useful to mention another woman who supported a scheme that could have had damaging effects on the Muslim community. 'Alī reports: "The Prophet sent me, together with al-Zubayr and al-Miqdād, and said to us: 'Go up to Rawḍat Khākh where you will find a woman travelling in a howdah. Take from her a letter she is carrying.' We went at high speed until we reached the place and we found the woman. We asked her to give us the letter, but she said that she had no letter. We said to her: 'You shall give us the letter or else we shall undress you' She undid her hair and gave us the letter she was hiding. We took it to the Prophet. It was a letter from Ḥāṭib ibn Abi Balta'ah to certain unbelievers in Makkah, telling them of the Prophet's march. The Prophet turned to him and said: 'Ḥāṭib, what is this?' He said: 'Messenger of God, please do not be quick to judge me. I was affiliated to the Quraysh, belonging to none of its clans. Your companions who had migrated from Makkah have their relatives who are certain to protect their families and properties. As I lacked such a connection, I thought that I could do the Quraysh a favour so that they would not harm my family. I have not done this as a result of being an unbeliever or accepting unbelief after I have been a Muslim'. The Prophet said to his companions: 'He has told the truth.' 'Umar said: 'Let me chop off the head of this hypocrite.' The Prophet said to him: 'He took part in the Battle of Badr. What would you say if God has looked at those who fought at Badr and said to them, "Do as you like, for I have forgiven you all."'" (Related by al-Bukhari and Muslim)

We may also consider lessons from earlier messengers and prophets. Noah's wife and Lot's wife persisted with unbelief, letting down their husbands and joining the ranks of unbelievers. God tells us in the Qur'an: "God has given examples of unbelievers: Noah's wife and Lot's wife. They were married to two of Our righteous servants but betrayed them. Their husbands could be of no avail to them against God. They were told: 'Enter both of you the Fire with all those who will enter it.'" (66: 10)

Principle Three:

> The education curriculum of Muslim girls should include basic information on the political conditions of their society, and should help them to develop an interest in such matters in preparation for adulthood. It should also make them fully aware of the role they, as women, must play in the political field. This includes:

- Taking part in expressing views on public affairs by different means such as writing, demonstrating or any other suitable method;
- Giving advice and exercising the right of support or objection. In other words, exercising the duty of enjoining right and forbidding wrong;
- Giving support to the political party or group whose programme is likely to serve the best interests of society;
- Supporting the candidate who is most likely to properly discharge the responsibility of representing the community.

In other words, exercising the right to vote in favour of the best candidate;

- Contesting parliamentary elections when a woman feels able to represent the Muslim community or a section of it.

It is also extremely important to teach girls how to utilise their spare time in good endeavours. Needless to say, taking interest in political developments so as to develop one's political vision that aspires to ensure fairness to all people is a good endeavour.

At this point, it is useful to discuss the practical aspects of women's participation in political activities, particularly their right to vote and to contest in parliamentary and other elections.

1. Women's Right to Vote: A Discussion

The discussion here focuses on two main points: establishing women's right to vote and the conditions that may be attached to exercising this right.

On the first point, we should first recall the fundamental rule that 'Everything is permissible unless ruled otherwise'. Since we do not have a Qur'anic or hadith text forbidding women's voting, we consider that it is essentially permissible. When it comes to practice, we take any permissible matter that is suited to our circumstances and serves our interests. It is useful to quote here a view expressed by the late scholar Muṣṭafā al-Sibā'ī, a former professor of Islamic law and dean of the Faculty of Shariah at the University of Damascus. This view is the conclusion of a discussion between a number of Islamic scholars on the question of women's right to vote and their right to stand for parliamentary election. He said:

> Having gone into a detailed discussion, we concluded that Islam does not forbid extending the right to vote to women.

> Voting is a method by which the community chooses representatives to enact laws and monitor the government's performance. Thus, voting is a method of appointing deputies. We go to balloting centres to vote for those whom we wish to be our representatives, speaking for us and defending our rights. Islam does not debar women from choosing such deputies to defend their rights and to express their views as citizens...[33]

The second point concerns any conditions that may be attached to women's exercising their right to vote. The main discussion has centred around whether a woman should have attained a certain standard of education, enabling her to form her own views independently from her husband or father.

Essentially, it was considered that there is no need for such differentiation between men and women concerning their voting rights, except perhaps in closed societies where women are denied any form of participation in social life and are kept totally isolated from men. Only in such a community should a gradual approach perhaps be advisable. In a more open society, where women enjoy a good measure of participation in the community's social life, there is no need for a stage-by-stage approach. The actual practice of voting will bring several factors into play, which will lead, year after year, to clear changes in the different mentalities of uneducated women who wait for a lead from their fathers or husbands, ordinary people who take their cue from tribal chiefs or notables, as also those who traditionally stand for election to represent the community. There will inevitably rise new figures and new parties, with new ideas and policies. They will play a part in enhancing people's awareness, men and women. Thus, it is through practice that men and women shall

---

33. Al-Sibāʿī, Muṣṭafā, *Al-Mar'ah bayn al-Fiqh wal-Qānūn*, Damascus, (n.d.), p. 155. – Author's note.

steadily improve their awareness of their community's needs and develop independent views and exercise free choice on the basis of what they determine to be in line with their beliefs and to serve their legitimate interests.

2. Women's Right to Stand for Election: A Discussion

> Again, the discussion focuses on two main points: establishing women's right to be elected and the conditions that may be attached to exercising this right.

i. *The woman's right to be elected:*

Let us once more remember the fundamental rule that makes everything permissible unless specifically pronounced otherwise. Since there is neither in the Qur'an nor in the Prophet's statements any text to outlaw women's election to parliament, then electing women is essentially permissible. When it is a question of practice, we may choose what suits our circumstances and serves our interests. Another quotation from the late Muṣṭafa al-Sibāʿī is particularly useful here:

> Since Islam does not prohibit women from voting, the question arises whether there is anything that prevents women from being elected to parliament. Before answering such a question, we need to understand the nature of the role of parliamentary representatives. This role has two basic functions: enacting legislations and monitoring government actions.
>
> As regards the first function, nothing in Islam debars women from taking part in the enactment of legislation, which requires, first and foremost, a high standard of knowledge and a proper awareness of the needs of the community. Islam gives men and women equal rights to

acquire knowledge. In our history, many women distinguished themselves as scholars of Hadith, *Fiqh*, Literature and other disciplines.

The monitoring of government action is basically an exercise of enjoining right and forbidding wrong. In this regard, Islam assigns equal rights and duties to men and women. God says in the Qur'an: "The believers, men and women, are friends to one another: They enjoin what is right and forbid what is wrong." (9: 71) On this basis we can say that nothing in Islam deprives women of the right to be a member of parliament, doing both functions of enacting legislation and monitoring government action.[34]

Thus, Professor al-Sibāʿī clearly concludes that Islam considers women fully qualified to be members of parliament. However, he felt that it was advisable that women should not exercise that right, for reasons relating to the interests of society.[35] This was a personal view looking at the social traditions prevailing in his home country, Syria, at the time. Needless to say, interests of society may change from time to time and place to place, and scholarly views on what serves such interests may differ.

Dr. Yusuf al-Qaradawi refutes the arguments of those who are opposed to women's election as members of parliament. Moreover, he differs with al-Sibāʿī on the advisability of such election. He feels that women's election to parliament will definitely serve the interests of society.

34. Ibid, p. 156.
35. Muṣṭafā al-Sibāʿī died in 1964. Syria gained its independence in 1946. From that date until his death, Syria was troubled by a series of military coups that ended the brief periods of democratic government the country enjoyed. He was a member of parliament in one of these periods (1949–1951).

Some people argue that membership of parliament bestows an authority over men, while women are not entitled to have such an authority. In fact, they say, the Qur'an makes clear that it is men who are in charge of women. How can we do the contrary and place women in charge of men? I would like to point out two things: the first is that the number of women who contest parliamentary elections is always small. The great majority which will always continue to make the decisions will remain in the hands of men. Hence, the claim that women's election will give them authority over men does not stand. Secondly, the Qur'anic verse that places men in charge of women speaks of family life. The man is the head of the family who is responsible for its wellbeing. The verse states: "Men shall take full care of women with the bounties with which God has favoured some of them more abundantly than others, and with what they may spend of their own wealth." (4: 33) The mention of spending is a clear indication of the area to which this statement applies, which is clearly the family. Indeed, this refers to the step or the advantage men have over women, mentioned in another Qur'anic statement: "Women shall, in all fairness, enjoy rights similar to those exercised against them, although men have an advantage over them." (2: 228) As for exercising a measure of authority by some women over some men, outside the family, there is nothing to preclude it. What is precluded is for a woman to be the overall leader.

Al-Bukhari relates a hadith in which Abu Bakarah quotes the Prophet as saying: "A community that assigns their affairs to a woman shall not be successful." This hadith speaks of the overall leadership, i.e. being the head of state. This is clearly indicated by the usage of 'their affairs', meaning top leadership in all matters. When it comes to authority in a particular area, there is nothing to preclude women. Thus, a woman may exercise authority in issuing fatwas or rulings, education, hadith transmission, management, and she may also exercise scholarly discretion and reasoning, or *ijtihād*. This is universally agreed upon by all scholars and women exercised such authority throughout all generations. Indeed, Abu Ḥanīfah considers that a woman may be a judge in any case in which she may be a witness. This excludes cases of mandatory and retaliatory punishments. However, Ibn al-Qayyim mentions in his book *al-Ṭuruq al-Ḥukmiyyah* that some scholars of old times maintained that she might be a witness in such cases. Both al-Ṭabarī and Ibn Ḥazm also sanction this, which means that there is no clear text that precludes women from being judges. Had there been any, Ibn Ḥazm, who is a strong advocate of taking every text at face value, would have firmly held to it. The occasion on which the Prophet said this hadith confirms that it relates to overall leadership. The Prophet was informed that after the death of their emperor, the Persians chose his daughter Burān to succeed him. He said: "A community that assigns their affairs to a woman shall not be successful."

Another point raised by opponents of women's election to parliament is their assertion that a member of parliament holds a position that is higher than the government and indeed higher than that of head of state. Her membership of parliament means that she can question the government and the head of the state. Thus, we prevent women from holding a position of overall authority, but we allow them the very same thing in a different way. To answer this objection, we need to explain the role of a member of parliament. It is well known that in all modern democracies, parliaments exercise a dual role of government accountability and legislation. When we look carefully at these functions we arrive at the following conclusion:

When carefully examined according to Islamic principles, accountability falls within what is known in Islamic terminology as 'enjoining what is right and forbidding what is wrong', and 'giving good counsel'. This is a duty Muslims owe to their leaders and to their fellow Muslims. It is incumbent on all men and women. The Qur'an clearly states: "The believers, men and women, are friends to one another: They enjoin what is right and forbid what is wrong." (9: 71) Since it is perfectly right for a woman to give counsel, express her views on what is right and what is wrong, enjoining the first and forbidding the second in her individual capacity, how can this same right be denied her as a member of an assembly that is required to exercise this function? In all matters of traditions and transactions, everything is permissible unless expressly forbidden in a clear religious text. It may be said that historical precedence in all Muslim communities shows that women were not members of any consultative counsel. To start with, this is not acceptable as evidence in support of women's exclusion. Besides, this is a matter that may be subject to different rulings according to social developments. Moreover, early Muslim societies did not exercise consultation through properly constituted counsels of either men or women. Indeed, we find that Islamic texts pertaining to consultation remain general, subject to interpretation by scholars according to changing circumstances.

The other function of parliaments is to enact legislation. Some people tend to exaggerate the importance of this function, claiming that it is more serious and far reaching than the position of head of state. It is the parliament which enacts laws for the state. Hence, they claim that it is not permissible for women to be involved in such a function. The matter is much simpler than that. In Islam, basic legislation belongs to God only. The principles that govern the enactment of law in Islamic societies are laid down by God Himself. All that we do as human beings, is to deduce rulings on matters that are not subject to any clear text and to provide details on questions to which some texts, expressed in general terms, apply. In other words, we exercise scholarly discretion, or *ijtihād*, in construction and deduction of rules. Such *ijtihād* is open to men and women alike. No scholar has ever suggested that being a male is a condition for the exercise of *ijtihād* by scholars. Besides, there are questions that relate to women and family relations in which women's views must be taken into consideration. Indeed women may have better insight into such matters than men. Examples of these may be found in the fact that ʿUmar ibn al-Khaṭṭāb accepted women's views on the inadvisability of setting an upper limit for women's dowries, the length of a husband's absence in war before the marriage is dissolved and giving child benefit on birth rather than weaning.

Having said this, we should add that a woman's membership of parliament does not give her any right of an unrestricted mixing with men. Nor should she sacrifice the rights of her family or disregard the values of Islamic morality. All these must be properly observed.[36]

Dr. al-Qaradawī further says in his ruling that it is a duty of Muslim women of piety to contest parliamentary elections so as not to give women of un-Islamic orientation a free field. A social or political need may be far more important than a personal need, which is acknowledged as a legitimate reason for a woman to play a role in public life.

---

36. Al-Qaradawī, Yūsuf, *Fatāwā Muʿāṣirah*, or Contemporary Rulings, Dar al-Wafa', Egypt, 1993, Vol. 2, pp. 376–382. (Summarized). – Author's note.

ii. *Conditions relating to women standing for election*

Some people ask whether the right to nominate female candidates should be limited to women's institutions or organisations in which women constitute a significant proportion such as professional associations, trade unions, social and cultural societies. This means that female members of parliament should only represent large sectors of women voters.

Extensive discussions of this question revealed that there is no need to make such a distinction between men and women, except perhaps in closed societies where women are denied any form of participation in social life and kept totally isolated from men. Only in such a community should a gradual approach perhaps be advisable. In a more open society where women enjoy a good measure of participation in the community's social life, there is no need for a stage-by-stage approach. However, when this is put into practice, it is important to conduct studies that indicate the areas in which female representation is more useful.

As for the values Dr. al-Qaradawī maintains that female members of parliament should observe restricted mixing, decent attire and the fulfilment of family duties, these are common values that must be observed by all women when they meet men in any area of society. We have devoted a complete chapter to the discussion of these values in this book.

Principle Four:

> Every woman is encouraged to spend of her own money, or her family's money in a reasonable way to support political activity, whether it is a duty or recommended. Her husband is recommended to help her when she is burdened with recommended political activity. If such activity is deemed to be a duty, helping her becomes his

duty. A husband shares God's reward for his wife's political activity, and his reward is increased according to the degree of encouragement and help he provides her with.

We have already cited evidence encouraging women to spend out of their families' budgets, and encouraging husbands to provide help for their wives when we discussed Principle Eight relating to women's social activity (Chapter 2 in this volume). The same applies here.

Principle Five:
Al-Nuʿmān ibn Bashīr quotes the Prophet as saying: "In their mutual compassion, friendly feeling and sympathy, believers are like one body: if one organ suffers a complaint, the whole body shares in sleeplessness and fever." (Related by al-Bukhari and Muslim)

A Muslim society is by nature based on mutual care and compassion. Good people in Muslim societies should always cooperate in:

1. Encouraging women to make a good contribution in the political field, making full use of the media to explain women's political role and responsibilities. Men should also be encouraged to help women to participate fully in politics;
2. Calling on political parties to establish sections and committees for women to enable them to take part in certain fields of their work, in addition to the areas in which they are active alongside men.

Principle Six:

Every Muslim government is required to ensure women's participation in political activity and to encourage such participation.

ʿAbdullāh ibn ʿUmar quotes the Prophet as saying: "Every one of you is a shepherd and accountable for those under his care. The ruler is a shepherd and he is responsible for his subjects". (Related by al-Bukhari and Muslim) This responsibility can be fulfilled in a variety of ways, including:

- Using the media, which is normally under government supervision to encourage women to contribute to the progress of society through full participation in political activity.
- Facilitating for women the exercise of their political role, making the right to vote in and contest, parliamentary elections universal to all men and women and giving women in particular the right to represent institutions that are limited to women or in which women constitute a significant proportion.
- Assigning a number of seats in local and legislative assemblies to women either by election or nomination.

Principle Seven:

> When women's participation in political activity necessitates their meeting with men, both men and women must observe the Islamic values of propriety already outlined when we discussed women's participation in social life. These include decent attire, lowering one's gaze, avoiding congestion and situations where one man meets one woman in an enclosed area and avoiding all other situations that raise suspicion.

Assuming that some existing political institutions do not observe these values, is it appropriate that the interests served by such institutions should be discarded through Muslim women's refusal to participate in them? Or should we give priority to ensuring these interests while we try hard to bring about the observance of Islamic values? The fundamental Islamic principles require us to balance needs and benefits against resulting harm and to weigh pros and cons in every situation. In this connection, Ibn Taymiyyah says:

- When we consider a resulting detriment that may require the prohibition of something, we must also consider the need that may encourage making it permissible, desirable or even required.
- Whatever is outlawed to prevent detriment should be permitted when it ensures serving clear interests. Islam disapproves of one man and one woman being alone in an enclosed space or travelling together and disapproves of a man staring at a woman because all these may cause detriment. Islam prohibits a woman from travelling unless she is accompanied by her husband or a close relative. Yet all these prohibitions are put in place because of the detriment they cause. Should there be a preponderant interest dependent on such matters, they are deemed not to lead to detriment.
- It is a rule of Islamic law that when something leads to mixed results, consideration is given to what is more likely.

A Testimony of a Contemporary Experience

In his book *Perestroika*, the former Soviet leader Mikhail Gorbachev has the following to say about women's emancipation in Western society:

> The extent of women's emancipation is often viewed as a yardstick to be used in judging the social and political level of society. The Soviet state put an end to the discrimination against women so typical of tsarist Russia with determination and without compromise. Women gained a legally-guaranteed social status equal with men. We are proud of what the Soviet government has given women: the same right to work as men, equal pay for equal work and social security. Women have been given every opportunity to get an education, to have a career and to participate in social and political activities. Without the

> contribution and selfless work of women, we would not have built a new society nor won the war against fascism.
>
> But over the years of our difficult and heroic history, we failed to pay attention to women's specific rights and needs arising from their role as mother and home-maker, and their indispensable educational function as regards children. Engaged in scientific research, working on construction sites, in production and in the services, and involved in creative activities, women no longer have enough time to perform their everyday duties at home – housework, the upbringing of children and the creation of a good family atmosphere. We have discovered that many of our problems – in children's and young people's behaviour, in our morals, culture and in production – are partially caused by the weakening of family ties and a slack attitude to family responsibilities. This is a paradoxical result of our sincere and politically justified desire to make women equal with men in everything. Now, in the course of perestroika, we have begun to overcome this shortcoming. That is why we are now holding heated debates in the press, in public organizations, at work and at home about the question of what we should do to make it possible for women to return to their purely womanly mission.[37]

I do not think that women's returning to their purely womanly mission would deprive her of the chance to do professional work or to participate in social and political activity. All it means is that there is urgent need to achieve the right balance between the woman's primary mission with her family and at home, and her other opportunities and missions.

---

37. Gorbachev, Mikhail, *Perestroika: New Thinking for Our Country and the World*, Harper and Row Publishers, New York, 1987, p. 118.